Straight
from the
Heart

Ken R. Burton

Kerby Publishing
Company Inc.

Kerby Publishing Company Inc.
Box 83055 Canyon Meadows P.O.
Calgary Alberta Canada T2W 6G8
(403) 253-1903

Design and production by Full Court Press Ltd.
Printed & Bound in Canada by D.W. Friesen Ltd.
for Kerby Publishing Company Inc.

Medical documentation in a book such as this is a collection of information that has been compiled through years of research by competent professionals in the medical field. This, unfortunately, is not a guarantee that all material is without error. Medical descriptions and diagnostic techniques described herein are correct to the best of the writer's knowledge, but no responsibilty is assumed for results obtained through their application.

Canadian Cataloguing in Publication Data
Burton, Ken R.
Straight from the heart
ISBN 0-9696903-0-4
1. Burton, Ken R. (Ken Ross), 1929– —
Health. 2. Heart—Diseases—Patients—Biography.
I. Title.
RC672.B82 1993 362.1'9612'0092 C93-091243-8

Acknowledgements

A book of this sort could not have been written by a person with my background without substantial technical input by professional people who graciously devoted their time and effort. Family and friends not in the medical field were also most helpful. Some contributed their experiences, and others helped by reading the manuscript, passing on comments even when the book was in its infancy. Their kind assistance helped me continue.

I want to thank all these people for this support. They include: cardiovascular surgeons T. M. Kieser and V. Aldrete of Calgary, Alberta, and T. R. Mycyk of Saskatoon, Saskatchewan; registered nurses J. Stewart, F. Hintze, P. Tan, K. Mierau and C. MacDonald; dietitian M. Toone, all of Calgary; Bob and Betty Sterling, Betty Sharp, Alana Knoke, Carol O'Grady, John Skelton, Tracey Ginn, Orie Mandryk, Jerry Pitts, Marilyn McIntosh, Pat Holmes, Gary Goral, Murray Feddema and Helen Smith; my wife, Marion, children Doug and Barb, and my sister-in-law, Betty.

I also thank Brian Brennan and Steve Roberts of the *Calgary Herald,* and credit the following publications and associations that assisted in my research: the *Calgary Herald,* the *Calgary Sun, Macleans,* The Heart and Stroke Foundation of Canada, The American Heart Association and the Cardiac Rehabilitation Program for Southern Alberta.

Jim Beckel of Friesen Printers was always available for that needed information or service that a novice requires, for which I am grateful. Last, but not least, I thank the people at Full Court Press who handled production and ensured that *Straight from the Heart* is the book I'd imagined it would be.

–Ken R. Burton
February, 1993

Contents

Dedication

This book is dedicated to the memory of
Dr. Harry Brody

Dr. Brody was head of the departments of obstetrics and gynecology at the Foothills Hospital and the University of Calgary medical school.

Born in Edmonton, Alberta, he graduated in medicine from the University of Alberta and completed his obstetrical training in Akron, Ohio.

Dr. Brody had a massive heart attack just prior to his 43rd birthday and passed away on October 18, 1975. He lectured extensively throughout the world, and shortly before his demise had completed a two-month lecture tour at the University of Saigon.

There are three children in the Brody family: Mark, a neurologist specializing in strokes and headaches, and now living in San Diego; Debra, married and residing in Calgary, has one son named Michael; and Mitchell, an MBA graduate now employed in Toronto, Ontario.

Betty (his wife) has since remarried—she and her husband Jack Sharp, a widower from Regina, Saskatchewan, now divide their residence between Calgary, Alberta, and Palm Springs, California.

Number One Killer

Heart and blood vessel diseases claim the lives of approximately 80,000 Canadians each year. Over 3,000,000 Canadians still suffer from these diseases. Forty-three percent of Canadians die because of this killer. In the United States, these figures are even more startling. 68,090,000 Americans are currently estimated to have one or more forms of cardiovascular disease (CVD). CVD claimed 982,574 lives in the U.S.A. in 1988. Nearly one-fifth of all people killed by CVD in the U.S.A. are under age 65. It is likely that heart disease or stroke will kill someone you know. It can strike suddenly, in the prime of life.

These statistics make many people aware that heart disease and stroke are the most frequent illnesses encountered. As well, they alert them to the frightening prospect that they could contact them. When informed that I was to undergo a triple bypass heart operation, the emotional trauma of the event devastated me. After the operation, I completely turned this feeling around. As my knowledge of heart-related illnesses increased, and my association with cardiac-oriented personnel grew, my outlook on life became much more optimistic.

If you have been subjected to heart disease, whether as a patient, a relative or friend of a patient, I believe this book will help you feel less apprehensive and hopefully help you avoid the emotional letdown experienced by the majority of individuals associated with a heart problem.

After I went through open-heart surgery, I had the strongest and strangest need, an almost spiritual one, to get the word out to others about my experience. The operation was not nearly the traumatic experience I had expected, and I felt then as I do now—that helping others to understand the process would reduce their instant fear of the words "heart disease."

After visiting many cardiac patients in hospital, I found most were looking for help from someone who had gone through a similar experience. It was then that I decided that I could reach many more by writing a book advising patients and other concerned people on various heart problems and describing the treatments as well as the feelings encountered while going through these curative measures.

I was not alone in this supposition. I have had assistance from three cardiovascular surgeons, six registered nurses and one dietitian in compiling this manuscript, all of whom were enthused at the prospect of such a book being written by a non-medical person who has gone through such an experience. Comments from these medical professionals are that they can pass on medical information about what the patient is about to face, but they cannot relate to the ordeal emotionally. They state that having such information available will help fill this void in their association with patients.

This book delivers a strong message to the medical world. The special bond between medical professionals and their patients, which is missing at times, is discussed in *Straight from the Heart.*

Hopefully, the goals I set by writing this book have been accomplished.

Matters of the Heart

I have talked about writing this book for over two years now, ever since the successful completion of my operation for a triple bypass. Tonight, I have just come from the Foothills Hospital in Calgary, Alberta, where a large group of volunteers, who will be canvassing for the Heart and Stroke Foundation of Alberta in another week, gathered to visit some of the cardiac facilities at the science center. The Foothills is a medical research hospital associated with the Faculty of Medicine at the University of Calgary. A portion of the funds collected by the heart fund canvassers is directed to this hospital for cardiac research.

While at the hospital, one of the speakers I encountered was a woman whose charisma pushed me from procrastination to action. This woman was not a public speaker or a PR spokesperson for the hospital or heart fund, but a cardiovascular and thoracic surgeon. In layperson's language, she performs heart operations as well as operations in the area of the body between the neck and the abdomen (the cavity in which the heart and lungs lie). Her name is Terry Kieser. Dr. Kieser gave us a brief introduction to the procedures used in heart surgery. The manner in which she described this crucial operation drew the attention of everyone in the group, from the time we walked into the room until it was time to leave. She also narrated the history of heart surgery from its inception to the present time, complete with explanatory descriptions. In one instance, Dr. Kieser referred to the TV program *Star Trek,* (which her four-year-old daughter watches faithfully), hopeful that some day heart surgeons will develop the same methods used on the program that now, in our world, require precise and, in some cases, drawn-out procedures. ZAP! Problem found: three blocked arteries. ZAP! Problem solved: arteries clear. All kidding aside, with the research and advancement in the cardiovascular field, the present procedures used for treatment in this field are improving to a point that was not even visualized a short time ago.

I find a certain confidence associated with the majority of the medical staff connected with heart problems. They not only display what seems like godlike characteristics, but they also project a type of humour that makes you wish that you were part of their everyday lives. The emotional stress a heart patient undergoes must in some manner trigger this response in these medical professionals.

I have, since my surgery, grabbed any booklet, periodical, etc. that I could get my hands on to learn more about the heart and the reasons for the various malfunctions that occur with it. It never occurred to me until the other day, when I received *Heart Health,* a periodical published by the Heart and Stroke Foundation, how people are concerned not only with their own problems but also with how the illness affects their loved ones. A woman asked a question in this periodical that seemed so simple to me that my immediate reaction was—Why don't you look up the answer in a medical book, and if you don't have one then go to the library where the answer to your query is readily available? Then I thought: This woman is not only interested in the medical procedure used for her husband's sickness, but she is also a concerned person reaching out with anxiety. She is wondering what will happen to her husband physically and how his illness will affect both of them emotionally. Her question was: "My husband suffers from angina, and his doctor has talked about 'angioplasty' as a possible solution. What exactly does it involve? What are the risks?" As I stated, this woman can get an answer to what angina and angioplasty are in a medical book, but it won't relieve what is most on her mind: "What is going to happen to my husband that will alter our lives, and what are the dangers to him?"

In this book, I attempt to answer this woman's question and bring you into the world of cardiac problems and solutions in everyday layperson's language. It not only describes the illness and its treatment, but also acquaints you with some of the feelings of those suffering from this malady and the effects of the illness on their family and friends.

Risk factors that brought on my heart problem are described and, where appropriate, ways to prevent this occurrence. Also narrated is: stress on the job and how, in some instances, it affects people physically and emotionally; about doctors and nurses, most of whom are dedicated to their profession and respected by their patients, and a limited few who aren't; about the feelings of the Nursing Unit Director of the cardiac unit at the Holy Cross Hospital in Calgary when she first entered this field of medicine; about my own experience with an angiogram; I was fortunate enough not to have had a heart attack, but a registered nurse will describe her feelings about this traumatic event, what she went through physically, and how it affected her and her family emotionally, and, as well, this medical professional describes her experience of going through angioplasty treatment; about the experience of a man who had his defective aortic valve replaced by a pig valve; about my ups and downs before and after open-heart surgery; about the cardiovascular surgeon and the procedures used in the operating room during heart surgery; about the stopover at the Intensive Care Unit after the operating room and before going back to a regular ward; about the emotional affect of my heart illness on my family; about the affect of pets on people undergoing emotional and/or physical problems; about two patients, one just about to undergo heart surgery, and the other who has had the same operation, and their feelings; about a fantastic rehabilitation program at the General Hospital in Calgary that is designed to regain the heart patient's confidence, as documented by the nurse who helped me through my rehabilitation; about diets and the way they relate to heart problems, as described by a dietitian in cardiac rehabilitation, complete with a list of heart-related cookbooks available on this subject; about a service of which few of us are aware—the Ladies Auxiliary and, finally, about using and understanding medical terms relating to the heart.

I had originally intended to name this book *Doc, I'm Scared!* However, I have found, as I go through the process of becoming an author, that such a title would direct this story to the autobiography sections in bookstores, where I'd be hidden behind Bill Cosby, General H. Norman Schwarzkopf or Madonna. With the present title, I hope it can hold its own in the Health and Fitness Section, and serve the purpose for which it was intended, to alleviate some of the apprehension of those associated with heart disease.

My initial inspiration to call the book *Doc, I'm Scared!* brought the exclamation from Marion, my wife, "You should have said frightened, not scared." However, she has not undergone open-heart surgery, and I can only comment to her that I was not only scared, but frightened, petrified, alarmed, appalled, devastated, irrational, unstable and any other such synonym that comes to mind to describe the barrage of feelings.

I am a 63-year-old who underwent triple bypass cardiac surgery three years ago on January 2, 1990. Before surgery, I was not just frightened, but terrified at the thought of going through the operation. Prior to surgery, I talked to everyone I knew who had heart problems, and the optimism the majority of these people displayed alleviated some of the tension I was undergoing. To say that I had no worries after discussing the operation with these people would be a lie—I still went into the operation with the feeling that this was it. After surgery, my whole outlook on heart-associated problems brightened. As I learned more and more about the function of the heart and the problems associated with it, I became more confident and understanding in this area.

I became a member of the Heart to Heart Support Society in Calgary. For a two-year period, I visited patients who were about to undergo cardiac surgery at the Holy Cross and Rockyview Hospitals in this city, or those who were recuperating after having had either a heart attack or heart surgery. These calls were meant to help alleviate some of a cardiac patient's apprehension. I now coordinate our Society's visitation program at these two hospitals.

It is essential when conversing with heart patients that we do not say anything that could affect their condition. Also, it is a prerequisite to evaluate whether the patient wants to be talked or listened to, or to be left alone, and just a limited few want the latter.

If I have helped any one person by visiting him or her while in the hospital, I feel that the time spent was in repayment to those who pacified me when I needed it. It would be gratifying if this feeling rolls on to others in the same manner, and they volunteer their services to help those who reach out for this type of helping hand.

I was fortunate to have stumbled across Larry King's

book, *Mr. King, You're Having a Heart Attack.* Reading this book before surgery and talking to those people mentioned above alleviated a lot of my fear about heart surgery. I know I seem to be talking in circles by saying that on one hand my fear was moderated, but on the other I was petrified before the operation. The only way I can justify this contradictory rationalization (don't attempt to interpret this phrase) is to say that you have to experience it to understand it.

Being a member of the Heart to Heart Support Society has enhanced my involvement in helping others. More heart-oriented support societies are now being formed in smaller centers. If you are undergoing any type of cardiac treatment, and have the opportunity to become involved in such a program, you will not only benefit yourself by doing so, but will be able to help others.

Words of Encouragement

Some of the doubts that kept entering my mind as I wrote this book were: Is it interesting enough that people would want to read it? Is the message I want to convey to others informative enough? Are the medical terms accurate yet not too technical for the average reader to understand? Does it lift up those people who need psychological inspiration at a point in their lives when such reassurance is so necessary?

Fortunately, through my association with the Heart to Heart Support Society and the Heart and Stroke Foundation of Alberta, these doubts have been alleviated by individuals I probably would have never met without such affiliations. Three of these people are Fran Hintze, Janice Stewart and Terry Kieser.

As stated in the opening, Mrs. Hintze had a heart attack on which she based pages 55 to 63—"The Road to a New Life: The Heart Attack" and "The Balloon Treatment: Angioplasty." Both Ms. Stewart and Dr. Kieser wrote letters after reading portions of this book and, as well, Ms. Stewart wrote pages 48 to 51: "We Fix Broken Hearts: The Cardiac Unit." The letters from these two medical specialists, as well as the one from my sister-in-law Betty Burton, gave me the inspiration to continue on and make an even more determined effort to complete this project when, at times, it began to lag.

One thing that I found so enlightening is that these women actually showed their appreciation and thanked me after I asked for their opinions on the manuscript. I felt I was imposing on them when asking for their help on this project. It is I who is expressing thanks and profound gratitude to them for the time and effort they took out of their busy schedules to assist me. Their act of caring shows what special people they are.

Janice Stewart attended the University of Manitoba and graduated with a Bachelor of Nursing degree. She is the Nursing Unit Director of Cardiology at the Holy Cross Hospital in Calgary, Alberta, and although she was not in this position at the time I underwent open-heart surgery, I now have occasion to be associated with her through my Heart to Heart visitations to the cardiac ward of this hospital.

This is her letter:

Ken:

I think this is a wonderful project that you've undertaken. This book comes "straight from the heart" and as such has several very attractive qualities. It's a nice way for you to express your experiences as a heart patient and to heal all the feelings, both pleasant and not so pleasant, about all that you have been through. I particularly enjoyed your style of writing; the way you talked right to the reader. I felt as if we were having a fireside chat instead of reading a third party account.

I enjoyed the way your message came across, that you were scared! I believe that message is very important for other people to hear who are undergoing similar experiences. I loved your honesty—both about the good and not-so-good moments. I can see appreciable benefits for future "heart patients" in reading your book in the early stages of their diagnostic procedures, and I can see appreciable benefits for families of "the patient" because they go through the experience, too.

You mentioned that your format is in the "rough stage" but I absolutely enjoyed reading it; thank you for the opportunity to do so. I am also very flattered that you have asked me to participate as a contributor, and I would be happy to do so.

Thanks, Ken.

Janice

Teresa M. Kieser completed two years of Honors Biology at the University of Western Ontario, joined the Canadian Armed Forces and at the same time continued her medical training. She interned in Toronto and, as the Canadian Government requires when going through university in this way, had to serve three years in the military after her graduation as a medical doctor.

Her goal in medicine was to be a surgeon, and as she did not relish three years of non-surgical service, she wanted to buy her release from the armed forces. When this was not possible, she agreed to work with a cardiologist at the National Defence Medical Center in Ottawa, and for two years saw heart patients. She did not become involved in surgery until her third year. She completed her training with a fellowship at the Ottawa Heart Institute.

Dr. Kieser started the Cardiovascular Surgery Unit at the Foothills Hospital in Calgary after moving from Ottawa in 1988, and is presently practicing cardiac surgery there. She performed her first full operation in 1984, after 14 years training and assisting in Ottawa and Toronto, and was the third woman in Canada to perform open-heart surgery.

Dr. Kieser is married and has two daughters, one born just two months ago.

Dr. Kieser's letter follows:

Dear Ken:

I want to sincerely thank you for letting me read your wonderful manuscript! There are a few minor things I have changed. All in all, I found it a very warm and touching account of how heart problems affect real people. You have a great gift. Your warmth and genuine sincerity comes shining through in your writing.

I did peruse, very quickly, the other book that you lent me to read; however, I found it much less personal, almost technical, like a medical textbook. I found delightful "God's Three Strays." I have an invalid mother who cares for three toy poodles, who feels exactly the same way about them that you did about your three little animals.

I also especially enjoyed your chapter "Peter and Dem: Different Patients, Different Feelings" and "Psychologically Speaking: How Are You Feeling?" I think it would be very wise for doctors and nurses to read your book as well, to realize the impact that they can have on patients.

Thank you very much for inviting me to read this manuscript.

Yours sincerely,

Teresa M. Kieser, M.D., F.R.C.S. (C)

Division of CVT Surgery

I was talking on the phone to my brother Jim and his wife, Betty, who live in Font Hill, Ontario, about this book and asked them if they would like to read the manuscript before I had it published and give me their opinion. Betty is an avid reader, and I told her that I definitely did not want words of flattery but her real feelings after she read it. Betty's response to this request was so beautiful that I want to share it with you.

Dear Ken:

I'm happy to say that I have finished your book (I don't mean that I'm happy to have finished reading it—but I'm happy to have read it). You've done a wonderful job of cataloguing your experiences, and reactions to them, and have made it very easy for those people for whom it was intended to understand it, and, I feel sure, to derive from it the help that you are offering to them.

It is very obvious that you have researched very thoroughly and have quoted from very reliable sources, and that fact alone should provide the peace of mind that heart patients are looking for. I feel, too, that your "chatty" style and your references to your own situation create confidence in your readers. In a nutshell, I'm sure that the book will give to those who need it and read it exactly what you are aiming for—a silver lining in what must seem a very dark cloud.

I sincerely hope that your expectations will be realized and that you will be successful in having your book published. We are both very proud and happy that you have taken a bad situation and turned it into something so very worthwhile, both for yourself and who knows how many countless others.

Congratulations and love from both of us,
Betty

Risk Factors in My Life

Risk factors that contribute to heart disease fall into one of two groups:

1. Those that cannot be changed—age, sex (men, at an early age, have a greater risk of heart disease than women), heredity, the presence of a heart problem and diabetes. Race is a consideration also because African Americans have a greater percentage of hypertension than whites.

2. Those that can be changed—smoking, high blood pressure and blood cholesterol levels, obesity, a sedentary lifestyle, and stress.

Karen Mierau, a nurse in the Cardiac Rehabilitation Program for Southern Alberta, has reviewed risk factors and some ways to reduce the incidence of heart disease on pages 131 to 135, "Towards a Healthy Lifestyle: The Next Step."

The risk factors listed above that contributed to my heart problem were age, smoking, heredity, obesity and last, but not the very least, stress. I had smoked cigarettes for approximately 20 years and then cigars for another 20, although I did quit about five years ago. The saying "Quitting smoking is the easiest thing in the world to do. I know; I've done it hundreds of times" certainly applied to me as I tried to kick the habit time after time. I did, however, finally reach a point in my life where I got completely fed up with smoking. During the last 20 years of this obnoxious habit, I had a cigar dangling out of my mouth from the time I got up in the morning until I went to bed at night. A pair of silk pajamas finally triggered a halt to the practice. My mother-in-law had given me a beautiful pair for Christmas, and during the festive season I was sitting reading the newspaper, puffing away as usual, when Boots (our loveable vagabond cat) jumped up on my lap and pushed the paper into the cigar, dropping ashes all over my pajamas and leaving a mass of holes. That did it! I decided then and there that it was finally time to quit. At the time, I did not know if I could keep this resolution, but to this day I have not had any desire to smoke again.

Presently, in our family, only my daughter Barb smokes and, although I would love to see her quit, I do not put any pressure on her to do so because I know what an ordeal it is to break this habit. In my opinion, the only way a person will quit is when, in his or her own mind, there is a desire to do so. When I think of going on holidays year after year, and driving along puffing away continuously, first on cigarettes and then on cigars, I now wish that I had never subjected my wife, son and daughter to the offensive habit of polluting them with side-stream smoke.

If you are a smoker and decide to quit (and for your own health it is certainly worth serious consideration) think of everything negative that you can about smoking—the smell of your breath, the stink of your clothes, the offensive odor in the air that others are exposed to, your health, the cost (not a hard thing to rationalize about these days), the possibility of fire, the increased cost of fire and health insurance, and any other derogatory thoughts that may enter your mind.

When you give up smoking, the outlook is very good. After four or five days without smoking, all nicotine is eliminated from your body. After one year, your risk of a heart attack is similar to those who never smoked.

The heredity factor for heart disease in my family is exceptionally high. In Haileybury, Ontario, when I was 16, I was alone one evening with my 60-year-old father when his head suddenly slumped over on his chest. I had no idea, at my age, what the reason was for his behavior and, although it was a cold February in Northern Ontario (about 30 below) and I was in my bare feet, I ran out of the house and over to the neighbors, barging into their house shouting, "Come quick; my dad's sick!" Two of the neighbor's daughters (in their 20s) dashed back to our house, and when they saw my dad, one remarked to the other "Call the doctor, Mr. Burton's dying!" They laid Dad on the chesterfield in the living room, and although Dr. Arnold got there a short time later, Dad had passed away. Ironically, he had nitroglycerin tablets in the pocket of his uniform (he was a provincial jail guard), but no one had ever told me about them, and I often wondered that if I had been taught what to do if he lost consciousness, and I had put a couple of those tablets under his tongue, whether his life could have been prolonged—only God knows the answer.

My oldest brother Bill passed away at the age of 57 in the early 1960s in Kirkland Lake, Ontario. He had one attack and came out of the hospital, but a second one proved fatal. Here again, if modern surgery had been available, he probably would have lived a much longer life.

My oldest sister Eva died of a heart attack on the sidewalk in New York city when she was only 49.

My second oldest brother Jack was living in Cobalt, Ontario, when at 65 he had a heart attack and died instantly after getting up one morning. My wife Marion received a call about Jack's sudden passing in the afternoon. When I came home from work, Marion waited until after we had eaten before passing on this disheartening message. She was concerned about my health at this time, and said later that she knew I would be in a more responsive frame of mind after I had the time to unwind from the day's work. I knew this was true and, after making the necessary arrangements for time off, flew back to Ontario for my brother's funeral.

My second oldest sister, Vina, who resided in Kirkland Lake, Ontario, died in her late seventies, and I believe she would have lived even longer but that she had a daughter Susan who died of an aneurysm when she was only 12. I think this tragedy shortened my sister's life, because she never had the same vibrant manner after Susan died.

My third sister, Muriel (although she was always known as Curly), who lived in Hawley, Pennsylvania, died in her mid-60s. This was the one member of the family who did not succumb to death by a heart problem, but by cancer.

My mother lived to be 88, and I like to think that I have inherited my mother's genes and, with the advantage of a bypass, will live to be a ripe old age.

Ever since my late twenties, I have been overweight, and although I am six feet tall, I weighed 247 pounds when I had the angina attack necessitating an angiogram. During the two months awaiting surgery, I managed to lose 20 pounds, which helped my physical condition for the operation, although if I could have lost more weight, it certainly would have been more beneficial. As you are probably aware, maintaining a healthy weight is an ongoing challenge to many of us.

The last, and again I emphasize not the least, of the risk factors is stress. In my opinion, this one risk factor accelerated my heart problem, and the diagnoses of two doctors proved I was not alone with this opinion. I will deal with this factor in the next chapter.

Stress in the Workplace

The oil patch used to be a fun place to work. When I was with Hudson's Bay Oil and Gas (HBOG), time after time I would look forward to the end of the weekend to return to my job. I felt a sense of accomplishment in life, and the effort I and others put into our work was rewarded by the way the company treated us. Unfortunately, the introduction of mergers turned this environment around.

Talk to any of many remaining in the industry today, and it's as though you're approaching a human time bomb—one ready to explode in frustration and anger. Walk into most companies, and it feels like you could cut the tension with a knife. Some workers put on a front, believing that they are the golden-haired employee who will convince management to keep them around. Co-operation and friendship between workers are on a downward trend, as one employee feels threatened by the existence of another, and all employees hope that if there is a lay-off, their co-worker's number will come up, and not their own.

The company I worked for publishes a weekly periodical on company activities. This brochure lists new employees, as well as those terminated. Although people were constantly being let go, new employees continued to show up on this list. It is evident that, in many cases, people where salaries had increased to an "expensive" level were being replaced by new personnel, who would receive less pay. After years of service to their company, employees were at an age where finding a comparable job was next to impossible, yet they were an expendable commodity in the eyes of their management. With children in school and a mortgage to pay, and sometimes with a spouse who was also laid off, frustration and devastation enter their lives. The stress from this scenario initiates, in many cases, a drastic psychological change that causes sickness and sometimes even death from either suicide or natural causes. If a person developed a heart problem, the stress from such a situation could initiate that fatal blow.

Calgary Herald writer Carol Howes has written several workplace articles that deal with stress. In these articles, she describes how large companies have a well-established procedure for terminating employees.

In larger companies, termination day is now routine. The procedure is well established—the employee about to be terminated is called into an office in the presence of his/her supervisor and a representative from human relations. The ordeal sometimes creates an emotional breakdown. Ironically, it is not always the employee about to be terminated that suffers this trauma, but one of the others. At times, outside professional help is used in an attempt to pacify these employees.

I have experienced instances where employees have been given notice of termination, and are kept around for a period of time. During this interval, different people react in different ways. I know of one employee who was given four months notice and was told that he would have to stay at his job for two months. During this two-month period, the employee would come in the morning, close his door, talk to no one all day, and leave at night. The company did not benefit from his two month continuance, and in this case, more harm was done than good. The company would have been much wiser to have paid the employee for the four months, and terminated him immediately.

After being advised of a lay-off, employees react in different ways. Some get drunk, some go into an emotional shell, some are not concerned and are quite happy to get away from a stressful situation, and some have even committed suicide. This last situation is usually kept low-key and only those very close to the demised person are aware of what happened.

Lay-offs continue. No sooner are people let go than some companies restructure again—looking for more terminations. This makes it extremely difficult for people to make any plans that involve a financial commitment—whether to buy a house, a new car, or even take a vacation.

Many companies now terminate in smaller numbers over a longer period of time, thus avoiding the publicity they were previously exposed to. Few people comment when they hear that such-an-such a company laid off one of two employees. The majority of the public is not aware, however, that this is occurring at frequent intervals, and this trend continues.

This whole scenario creates poor morale, a decline in productivity, increased stress, guilt and depression.

It's unfortunate that management, in their misguided wisdom, have promoted individuals, either one of their favorites, or someone who costs less money, who do not have the training and are incapable of doing the job they have been destined to fill. In most cases, this is not the fault of the employee, but it must reflect on the performance of the company. I, after a merger, had a supervisor who, although he headed up a business administration section, was inexperienced for his position. Here again, this situation is not the doing of this employee, and actually he was a likeable individual.

Two mergers in the oil industry affected my life in particular. In late 1981, Dome Petroleum acquired Hudson's Bay Oil and Gas, a business decision that was completely irrational and forced the financial ruin of the two companies. As seems to be the trend in these mergers, the majority of the supervisory positions are filled by the take-over company. Dome had an administrative drilling manager, the equivalent to my position at HBOG. This manager was much younger with lesser experience, but was assigned the new managerial position making, of course, my old position redundant. I was than given a routine inventory control assignment, work that a novice in the industry was capable of doing. After a six-month period of attending meetings and listening to Dome supervisory personnel constantly beating their own drums, trying to impress their subordinates of their importance to the operation, and attempting to convince their superiors of the critical role they played in it, I decided there was something better for me in the industry as well as in my own life.

Both Hudson's Bay Oil and Gas and Dome Petroleum no longer exist under these names. The companies I identify as "A" and "B" in the following are still in operation, and there is no added content to the story by identifying either one.

At 52 years of age, I made an exceptional stress-related decision. I resigned and went to work for Company "A." I got back into drilling as an administrative supervisor, coming back to the type of work I enjoyed.

In 1988, Company "B" took over "Company A." I was completely frustrated after this merger, and, although I was not laid off, I was demoted—told I was too old for my previous position and also firmly advised that I was overpaid in my present position and should not expect a raise during my remaining time with the company (the manager making this statement later denied it, of course; he probably had time to think over the consequences of his remarks). I was given a nothing job, possibly with the expectation that I would become disillusioned enough to resign. I am certain that my exposure to this situation at work accelerated my heart condition, and as I said earlier, medical evaluation strengthened this supposition.

For a financial inequity, I can give a no better illustration than to refer to a letter I received from J. Howard Macdonald, in reply to my request to have my pension reviewed—I had elected to take early retirement when I resigned from Dome Petroleum. I had written the letter after discovering that golden handshakes were given out a year after I left to a certain group of employees who would voluntarily take early retirement. These employees received an enhanced pension, whereas those of us who had already left, did not. HBOG had a pension plan in place, whereas Dome Petroleum issued stock to their employees in lieu of a pension plan. Thus HBOG had accumulated a fund that, in my opinion, should have been monies in trust for HBOG employees who were responsible for the accumulation of this employee benefit asset. I still believe there was an injustice done to a lot of retirees who had voluntarily retired earlier, and were not included in this bonanza. Macdonald's reply was that he could not approve any adjustment to my pension; however, and I quote from his letter: " I am pleased to inform you, however, that our Board of Directors recently approved a cost of living supplement to Dome's current annuitants. This increase will first be reflected in your September pension payment."

Macdonald's statement about this increase proved to be correct and I received an additional $3.27 a month! This increased my monthly pension from $506.19 to $509.46. I suppose that such a settlement wouldn't be quite so irksome if the CEO of Dome, J. Howard Macdonald, had taken on his share of the financial burden. The company did, however, manage to scrape together a little extra cash to keep Macdonald happy.

According to published newspaper reports, Macdonald's contract included the following:

1. an annual $500,000 U.S. salary that has risen sharply with inflation protection and merit increases.

2. $37,788 for loss of 'potential' benefits for going from Royal Dutch Shell to Dome. ·

3. payment of increased educational costs for his children.

4. payment of travelling costs to visit England for holidays.

5. a furnished home in Calgary for a "reasonable rent." This home was depreciated by 12.5 percent each year if he wished to buy it eventually.

6. payment of his moving costs back to England when the hiring pact ends in September 1988, or sooner if Dome's ownership changes hands.

7. a pension for life after age 60, which he's nearing, that guarantees an annual 120,000 pounds by making up the difference between his Shell pension (recently estimated at 69,000 pounds), with the total package rising annually with the erratic U.K. inflation rate.

8. an incentive option of 3,000,000 Dome shares that can be exercised at $5.875 until October, 1993. Though Dome's shares were 25.38 in 1981, they haven't been close to that exercise price for years. However, his contract also provides that he or his estate will receive at least $1 million cash for the options anyway, a no-lose "incentive." He later received another 10-year option for 1.5 million more shares at $2.75 apiece.

9. an additional benefit, effective March, 1985,

was that Macdonald will receive a lump sum payment of $1.5 million U.S. if Dome is taken over by Amoco or anyone else, disposes of most of its assets, if anyone acquires more than 20% or if ownership noticeably changes between Dome and Dome Mines Ltd.

Macdonald's remuneration sure looked better than my increased pension to $509.46 each and every month.

I do not blame Macdonald for accepting this windfall, but I certainly am critical of the people who create a system that gives one individual more remuneration than he can possibly use in a lifetime, while others are laid off in the prime years of their life, with families to support and who, in more instances each day, are unable to meet mortgage payments to keep a roof over their heads. Many of these unfortunates are at an age when the establishment doesn't want them anymore, and they are being replaced with younger and less expensive personnel, despite that inexperience is replacing experience and knowledge. No wonder stress is taking a greater toll on our health.

Psychologists have identified two types of behavior patterns: type A and type B—both of which can be related to susceptibility to stress and, therefore, heart problems. Type A people respond to physical and environmental challenges with a greater increases in their pulse rate, activity level and blood pressure than type B people. Type A people are characterized by high degrees of competitiveness, aggressiveness and awareness of time pressures. Type A persons have about twice the risk of a heart attack as type B persons; if you have had one heart attack already and are type A, you are more likely to have another one than type B people who have had a heart attack. Type A individuals are also more likely to have narrowing of their blood vessels; and the more type A characteristics people have, the greater their risks of a heart attack.

With the amount of continuous research being done

in this area, it has become somewhat apparent that type Bs (the relaxed, easy-going, contemplative, easily satisfied individuals who do not become angry or easily agitated) are also susceptible to the silent killer (the heart attack) because they suppress an inner tension which is at times ready to explode like a dormant volcano.

I am TYPE A in capital letters. I know it, that is why I have to find safe ways to vent my frustration. For example, much of what I originally wrote for this chapter will never appear in published form, but putting those thoughts on paper did help to alleviate my type A characteristics.

After I visited my cardiologist in November, 1989, he stated that I was not to return to work, and was to enter the hospital the next week for an angiogram. When the results of this test became known (that I would have to undergo bypass surgery), I advised my manager, stating that I would be down within the next week to get some things from my files. Before the week was up, one of my cohorts phoned me, stating that my supervisor was going through my office, and throwing out files. I came down immediately and discovered 30 years of accumulated administrative data (much of which I intended to retain) in the trash can. Contrary to venting my anger as would have been my usual characteristic, I had a feeling of complete resignation and disgust at the pillage being done, and turned and walked out.

STRESS IN THE WORKPLACE? You'd better believe it!

How Are You Feeling?

I sat in on an orientation session a nurse at the Holy Cross Hospital was giving to three men (accompanied by their wives) who were about to undergo heart surgery. This nurse made a statement that anyone facing this ordeal should think about: "Open-heart surgery is an extremely emotional period in your life, and your recovery is based on your attitude; and the proportion of the illness you are experiencing is about 10% physical and 90% mental." How true! Yet it appears that a few doctors (and a few nurses) have a complete disregard for the feelings of those in their care. If these personnel only realized that sometimes a patient requires a psychological lift, which could easily be administered by uttering a few reassuring words.

Most doctors are held in high esteem by their patients, while a limited few have mannerisms that make patients uncomfortable. Such mannerisms do not necessarily make these doctors' ability to treat people inadequate, but in my experience a charismatic approach to patients not only puts them more at ease and takes their minds off the pain they are suffering, but it also tends to shorten their recovery period.

When I encounter a doctor who turns me off or makes me feel emotionally uncomfortable, I terminate my association him or her immediately. Unfortunately, some individuals faced with this situation are either too timid to say or do anything, or they are prepared to accept the affiliation as it is for some other reason. Thank God, this type of doctor is in the minority.

I have encountered four doctors for whom I did not care, and I terminated any further relationship with them. Maybe they were just as glad to get rid of me but, frankly, I really don't give a damn. While these four certainly don't represent the majority of concerned medical professionals, my encounters with them were significant enough that I'd like to share them. Hopefully, they'll serve as a reminder that patients are more than assembled body parts.

When I was 19 and in the air force, I was in a motorcycle accident with a chum and sustained serious facial injuries, which included a broken jaw, lacerated tongue, and the loss of several teeth. During my recovery, my teeth had to be repaired, and the dental officer at R.C.A.F. Centralia where I was stationed was known for his indifferent approach and blunt manner towards his patients. On my first visit, he gave me an exceptionally hard time, and because I was still in much pain from the injuries, and had an aversion to going to dentists in the first place, I was practically a basket case when I left his office knowing had many more treatments to undergo. At 19 and away from home, I wasn't sure what to do, but I finally decided to talk to the SMO (Senior Medical Officer). This doctor was aware of the traumatic ordeal I had undergone in Westminster Hospital in London (I nearly died from loss of blood), so he granted permission to get treatment from a military dentist in London I had once been to when stationed there. This dentist had an outgoing, friendly disposition and when visiting him, the fear I had of dentists lessened considerably. I completed the necessary treatments and experienced none of the apprehension I had experienced with the dentist in Centralia. I often thought that if the Centralia based dentist did not clean up his act when he returned to civilian life, his practice would be very limited.

The second doctor on my I-don't-want-to-see-again list had taken over a practice from the doctor I had used ever since coming to Calgary in 1956. In that year, when I started to work in Calgary, it was necessary to have a medical. I always liked the company doctor who performed this task and accepted him as my physician. When this doctor retired some 20 years ago, he sold his practice and moved elsewhere. When I required medical treatment after he left, I was referred to the doctor who bought this practice and after one visit with him decided that there was some other doctor in my future. He had that brisk, abrupt, authoritative manner about him that immediately gave me an uncomfortable feeling. I do not know to this day anything about his professional ability, and I do not even remember his name, but I do know that I was not prepared to be treated by a person with his mannerisms.

Number three on my list was a cardiologist to whom I was referred when an attack of angina prompted the need for his services. When I went into his office, he had me get onto a treadmill and kept me on it for an uncomfortably long period, and the pain in my chest was becoming unbearable. I don't know whether or not his intention was to keep me at it until I had a heart attack, but I wasn't prepared to find out, and told him so.

This doctor had such a different approach from the cardiologist who attended me during the period I went through before and after my open-heart surgery. When stress-testing me on a treadmill, this cardiologist continuously enquired about any pain or shortness of breath, and when I finally did reply in the affirmative, stopped the test immediately.

Ironically, just yesterday I made one of my periodic visits to the Holy Cross and encountered a woman who was about to have a bypass operation. She had some complications (an infection), and until this cleared up the operation was put on hold, leaving her apprehensive while awaiting the oncoming operation as well as bored, a feeling that accompanies inactivity as an in-patient in the hospital. This type of person usually displays a noticeable feeling of depression. When I asked her who her cardiologist was, she mentioned doctor number three on my list. She said that she was not pleased with him and had told him with that she did not appreciate his rudeness. Her daughter, who was in the room when I visited, mentioned that her 34 year old brother had been this doctor's patient because of a heart attack. The doctor saw him one day in the hospital, and his diagnosis was that he lose 30 pounds and quit smoking. This man had never smoked in his life and was quite thin! His reaction was to change cardiologists, and although I certainly will not interfere with any patient's medical status, I was curious enough to ask her why she remained with this doctor when her son had changed, and she was obviously not happy with him. Her reply was that she had been through the period of time where her cardiologist would be making any further decisions before the oncoming operation on her medical condition, but she was considering this action. This, of course, was her prerogative, but I find it hard to understand why people subject themselves to this kind of treatment. I do think some of the reason is that many people are overly awestruck by their doctors, and are frightened to make a decision that would alleviate the problem. Her daughter does not have the same attitude, and it appears it is only a matter of time before she changes her mother's attitude as well.

The fourth and last doctor on this list (thank God there aren't any others) was the company doctor where I had worked. I decided to see her about some company benefits after I had been on disability for over a year. When I visited her at her office, she had no record of me being on disability, which was no fault of hers. Despite medical recommendations that I not return to work, she seemed more interested in questioning me about why I was on disability than in trying to assist me. During the course of my conversation with her, my family's medical history came to light, and her comment about it was: "With your family history of heart disease, you won't live to be that old anyway."

Talk about a psychological lift! This, of course, put her on my "if-I-ever-see-you-again-it'll-be-too-soon" list. She made me feel like I was gold-bricking, and during the course of our meeting she requested that I have a meeting with the manager of Human Resources to discuss my medical disability, despite that my doctor had recommended I not return to work.

She also asked if I wanted to see a psychologist. As I didn't think I had completely lost it, my immediate reaction was to turn down this request. It's unfortunate that many people have the wrong conception of this service, and for this reason do not use it. However, as the stress I was subjected to during take-overs and lay-offs put me on a sleeping pill and tranquilizer list for a long period, I gave more thought to the proposal after returning home. I then decided that this could be a way of letting management know some of the inequities that were occurring within the organization, and that it might give me a chance to unload some of the frustrations that were eating away at me.

Although I apparently never made any impact on management, it actually turned out to be one of the better decisions I could have made for my own peace of mind, because the psychologist I saw on the advice of this doctor confirmed my diagnosis. This, I felt, threw a monkey wrench at the company doctor's diagnosis. As well, it confirmed my disability, and I did not have to return to a stressful situation in the work force.

It is strange that I got to this part in my book last night, and when I picked up this morning's Calgary Herald, there was a letter to Ann Landers from a person who works in a cardiologist's office. This person (Monica) states that there are times when a patient scheduled for a stress test is kept waiting an unreasonable length of time until the cardiologist arrives. The law requires the presence of a cardiologist during this test (in Sarasota). Invariably, the patient vents his or her anger on the technical or nursing staff. Monica says that she tells these people to let the cardiologist know how they feel, but no one does. She says that even the most irate patient becomes a pussy cat the moment the doctor enters the room. The cardiologist will give the patient some excuse about an emergency somewhere, which is seldom the case. Ann's reply was that it's a fact of life that most patients in the doctor's waiting room need the doctor more than the doctor needs them. This tends to make some doctors arrogant and inconsiderate. She goes on to say that if a doctor is consistently more than 40 minutes late, the patient should tell him or her and not the nurse, receptionist or technician: "The long wait produces anxiety and anger. Please be more realistic about your scheduling or I will have to find another doctor." And then do it.

The attitude of the people mentioned above is predominant, and I agree with Ann Landers. If you are not getting the treatment you feel you deserve, or if you are going through an uncomfortable experience with your doctor, discuss it with him or her, and if you do not receive satisfaction, change doctors. There are so many good ones around.

Most people look after their cars better than they do their bodies. If people are unhappy with the way a mechanic services their car, they don't hesitate to change to another mechanic. Yet when the human body receives unsatisfactory service, people will, in many cases, either procrastinate or take no action at all to remedy the situation.

Nurses associated with heart surgery seem to have the same emotional approach to patients that most doctors have. With the exception of the brief encounter I had with a nurse at the Rockyview as discussed in the chapter "Different Patients, Different Feelings," I have had only one unpleasant association with a nurse, and that was during my recovery at the Holy Cross.

The nurses at the Holy Cross Hospital came into our room faithfully at 2:00 AM and, as the old story goes, woke us up so they could give us our sleeping pills. Of course, this is not really the case, as patients are scheduled for medication at periodic times during the day, and 2:00 AM is one of the times designated to obtain continuity in dispensing medicine. As well, it is an ideal time (near mid-shift) for nurses to check on the medical status of their patients. The nurse referred to above came into our ward one morning at 2:00, and I, along with my three roommates, was deep in slumberland. I did not require medication at this time so didn't anticipate being disturbed. With a pillow at the bottom of my bed and my feet hanging over—I was too long for the bed—I felt snug as a bug in a rug. You would think I had violated a cardinal rule of the establishment because the nurse woke me up and asked me why my feet were sticking out. When I told her the reason for this seemingly strange behavior, she asked me if I couldn't get a longer bed, or if I could curl up and tuck my feet in. At the time I couldn't understand her rationalization, as I didn't think they would deliver a new bed in the middle of the night, and I could not see why I should have to change positions for sleeping. Actually, she was quite indignant over all this, and then she went after another one of my roommates, about some other trivial matter and then left. I turned to another roommate, George Cairns, and remarked "It sure seems like somebody peed in her Corn Flakes this morning." I thought he would never quit laughing, and to this day, he still mentions it when we get together.

A knowledgeable professional later informed me that although she did not condone the method in which this nurse acted, the nurse, in all probability, had a perfectly good reason for enquiring about the way I was lying. Nurses are constantly trying to make sure that no pressure areas will obstruct the flow of blood back to the heart, causing blood clots to form—hence the reason you cannot cram your feet in a manner that will obstruct this flow. In everyday life it's fine because we are more active, whereas in the hospital, the patient may spend long periods in bed, not moving much.

I learned a lesson, and I hope the same message will be given to those who read this book and require medical assistance. Even though some of the requests you get from medical staff may seem completely irrational, there may be a perfectly legitimate reason for the request—which is not obvious to the patient being subjected to the ordeal.

At times, you may be apprehensive about some request while undergoing medical treatment. If this occurs, a suggestion is to discuss the situation with whomever is making the request, in an attempt to clarify the reason for it. If it is something of major concern and you are not satisfied with the answer you receive, I feel it would be appropriate to get a second opinion.

In all fairness to the staff, sometimes a patient can be over-demanding and a real pain in the rear, and I did have occasion to run into one while at cardiac rehabilitation. This person had a very short fuse, and he mentioned that at one time he did not get some immediate service to a request, so he picked up some piece of equipment and threw it across the room. If I were a nurse in this case, I imagine I would find it difficult to retain my composure at this time. Maybe the nurse that came into our room that morning had encountered some unpleasant experience with such a patient, and her temperament carried over to our room.

There are times when a medical professional's mannerism is completely acceptable to one type of person, and yet quite offensive to another. The only way to justify such behavior is if the professional was very familiar with the patient and knew what type of approach was suitable.

I have often thought that I would like to write a letter to that doctor who has a wonderful gift of healing but an offensive attitude.

Dear Doctor Heartless:

As you know, I have been under your care, and my medical illness has now been arrested and/or healed.

I was frightened and ill when I was referred to you. When I began to feel better, I looked upon you as my saviour. There were, during this time, moments when I was quite uncomfortable having you around. During my recovery, I would sit and wonder why such a gifted person could make me feel better in body but so uncomfortable in mind.

When you took "The Oath of Hippocrates," one of the passages you swore to uphold reads, "I will follow that method of treatment which, according to my ability and judgement, I consider for the benefit of my patients, and abstain from whatever is deleterious and mischievous." The meaning of the word *deleterious* to you, should be quite obvious. To me it was a word I had never seen before and which I did not, of course, understand. I did, therefore, check this word (which I thought must be very important to be included in this Oath) in two different dictionaries. To refresh your memory, one dictionary states this word means "to hurt; harmful often in a subtle or unexpected way," the other "harmful (to mind or body)." Perhaps you are not even aware that you are not conforming to this Oath.

No doubt at times you have patients who test your patience. In this situation, why don't you have a "Heart to Heart" talk with your patient. I may even be such a person, and if you spoke to me, I would either attempt to clean up my act and hope to improve the situation, or, if I felt the two of us had a personality conflict for which there was no solution, I would go to another doctor.

At other times, there may be intervals where you have not been to bed for countless hours and you are overtired. Maybe your practice is too large, and you just don't have enough hours in a day to handle it anymore. If this is the case, for the welfare of both you and your patient, why don't you cut back, or consider bringing an assistant into your practice? You're not doing either your patients or yourself any justice by attempting to be a martyr.

Well, Doctor, that's the way I feel. If the gift of healing you have was combined with the gift of compassion, what a wonderful service you would administer. Your patients would feel better and so would you.

Sincerely,

A grateful but unhappy patient.

It's difficult to direct derogatory remarks to those in the medical profession because the majority of personnel in this field do so much good, but it sure isn't any problem to eulogize them. I could name numerous doctors, nurses and other medical people with whom I have had the pleasure of being associated professionally. Some of these are:

Dr. Harry Brody (deceased)—I have dedicated this book to the memory of Dr. Brody. Unfortunately, he was taken from us in the prime of his life with a massive heart attack. He was the obstetrician who brought my son Doug into this world on November 26, 1964. He also attended Marion for five months when she was pregnant with Barbra. We were then transferred to Prince Edward Island, where my daughter was born in Charlottetown on May 21, 1970. On our return to Calgary, Marion continued to see Dr. Brody for post-natal check-ups.

Dr. Brody had a calm and gentle manner towards not only my wife, but also myself, that put both of us more at ease during her pregnancies. He always had that extra time to discuss concerns and ease our apprehensions. It was particularly a comfort knowing he was there because we were an older than average couple expecting a first child.

At times I wonder why God decides to take this type of person from us so early in life.

Dr. John C. Zubis—I was fortunate enough to have been referred to Dr. Zubis about 20 years ago by a friend of ours, Edie Greilach. Dr. Zubis has helped me through trying times, not only with my cardiac problems, but with other illnesses as well. He has an approach that puts me at ease and creates a feeling of complete trust in his medical capabilities. During the emotional trauma I underwent through layoffs and mergers, I am certain that his being there when I needed him prevented me from having even further psychological or cardiac complications. During the waiting time for my surgery (two months), I saw him every week as there was constant apprehension about the risk of my having a heart attack, and I was petrified at the thought of the upcoming surgery. I therefore would walk into his office time after time with the comment, "DOC, I'M SCARED!" His approach to this mental dilemma helped me through the drawn-out ordeal, and it is my wish that anyone subjected to this experience is fortunate enough to be associated with a person like Dr. Zubis. It's impossible to fully describe my feelings towards this doctor.

Dr. R. R. Singh—When I originally complained of pains in the chest area, I was referred to Dr. Singh. I am certain that Dr. Singh has long forgotten me, but I still think of him as one of the doctors I would like to have if the occasion arose. I was especially upset, because this was my first exposure to this traumatic illness, and he not only listened to my fears, but was extremely compassionate. Dr. Singh is a specialist in internal medicine, and for this reason I did not continue to see him when angina was diagnosed.

Dr. Victor Aldrete—the cardiovascular surgeon who performed my open-heart surgery. When I compared the medical association to deity, this is the doctor who gave me this thought. Here again, I agree with June Pimm's remarks that the heart has deep emotional significance, and after being operated on and knowing that my heart had stopped for a period of time, I feel there is a divine element to this procedure, and I associate it with Dr. Aldrete, who performed this function. Dr. Aldrete, even though he must go through a gruelling schedule with the pace he maintains, has a pleasant disposition and always has the time to explain the questions thrown at him. He also reassured me at a time in my life when this type of treatment was critical. Immediately after my operation, and although he could have just as easily designated the chore to an associate or not bothered to do so at all, he took the time to phone my wife Marion to tell her that the operation was a success and everything was okay. This was only one of the many special traits Dr. Aldrete displayed.

Dr. G. S. Attariwala—although not connected with the cardiac field (he is an eye specialist), this doctor also has a charismatic approach that makes him my choice for eye problems. He operated on my son Doug 25 years ago for a cyst on his eye. At the time, both Marion and I were pacified by Dr. Attariwala's mannerism during this emotional experience in our lives. He listened to our concerns, and his replies comforted us by his warmth and sincerity. With my present iritis condition, I do need the services of a specialist in this field. I feel very comfortable in having selected Dr. Attariwala for this treatment.

Janice Stewart—Registered Nurse—Janice is the Nursing Unit Director of Cardiology at the Holy Cross Hospital. Although she was not in this position when I was operated on, my present association with her, when I visit patients as a representative of the Heart to Heart Support Society, allows me to view firsthand the sensitivity she displays towards her staff and patients.

Fran Hintze—a Registered Nurse at the Rockyview Hospital, and, as stated previously, coordinated Heart to Heart visits at both the Holy and the Rocky. Because she has had a heart attack herself, Fran probably understands even more the emotional trauma of a cardiac patient, and her manner portrays this. She projects that feeling of caring that is so appreciative from someone with a heart problem. This projection is so important to those in need of help in this area.

Royal Srigley-Peters—a Registered Nurse in Dr. Zubis's office. Royal has that warm and cheerful way about her that makes you feel comfortable when visiting the doctor. She has worked for Dr. Zubis for a number of years, which is a plus for us who go there. Her attitude towards her job and approach towards patients puts her on this list of special professionals.

The nurses, dieticians, exercise specialists, psychological personnel, stress testing staff and all others connected with the cardiac rehabilitation program at the Calgary General Hospital—these professionals deal with patients who have gone through a traumatic physical experience with significant psychological effects, and they are to be commended for the manner in which they treat their patients. Their impact has directed a great number of cardiac patients towards a more fulfilling and enjoyable life than they thought would be possible before taking this program.

Last, but certainly not least, the nurses on the cardiac ward and in ICU at the Holy Cross Hospital—these nurses demonstrate a loyalty that is a credit to their profession, and their attitude towards patients makes recovery that much easier. I would think they must get an immense feeling of fulfillment from the good they do. If, at times, they do feel overtired or a bit down on the job, perhaps knowing the gratitude we heart-fixed alumni feel towards them will pick them up and give them that emotional lift they so often give us, their patients.

The Cardiac Unit

Walk onto the cardiac ward of any hospital, and you probably won't notice anything different or any change of atmosphere from any other hospital ward. You'll see nurses at what appear to be routine tasks—writing up reports, looking after the needs of patients, monitoring the progress of those under their care, talking to and advising doctors on a patient's progress or performing many of the day-to-day tasks needed to run the ward. Behind this picture of orderliness is a team of busy professionals who are trained to look after one of the most highly emotional type of patient there is—the heart patient. I speak for this type of patient, having been one myself, and the appreciation I have for what these nurses do cannot justifiably be put into words.

When I finally decided to write this book, one of the topics I wanted to include was how a nurse who worked on this ward felt. I approached a person who is as well-qualified to write on this subject as anyone I know. She graciously agreed to document some of the feelings of a nurse who is confronted with the responsibility for the physical well-being of those undergoing cardiac treatment.

This person is Janice Stewart, and, as described on page 18, she is the Nursing Unit Director of Cardiology at the Holy Cross Hospital in Calgary, Alberta.

Here is her story:

I remember the first time I set foot on a cardiac unit—I was nervous! As a student nurse, I was there to learn how to practice all the theory about heart disease that I had studied in class. My first impression of the staff was WOW! These people know so much and they seem to be so busy all the time. Frankly, I was intimidated and just a little shy.

I also remember the first patient I looked after. He was 42 and I admitted him to hospital for his bypass surgery. He was scared! This was the first time he'd ever had surgery of any kind, and this was the big one. He was so nervous that he asked not to be told anything about how the surgery is done. At first I had difficulty with that because I believed everyone not only had a right to know, but everyone should know what he or she was getting into. But, as I got to know him, I grew to understand and respect his choice. It was his way of coping with the stress of being in the hospital and waiting to go for open-heart surgery.

These memories and experiences I carry with me, and they have given me some insight into the people who arrive at the cardiac unit. Firstly, everyone is scared—no matter how they appear on the outside. They come, having to put their trust in a team of strangers, whose knowledge and experience will see them through their surgery. The team includes the doctors; the nurses on the cardiac unit, in the O.R. and the ICU; the physiotherapist; the social worker; the respiratory therapist; the occupational therapist; the dietitian and the pharmacist—all pulling together to "pull" the patient through from admission to discharge.

The team efforts on the cardiac unit are usually coordinated by the nurses, whose unique position provides them with the opportunity of getting to know the patient best. Cardiac patients come in all shapes, sizes and backgrounds, and although there is a common thread, each person is an individual with different needs. In my experience I have found that no two people go through their stay on the cardiac ward in the same way. However, having said that, some generalities can be made. Those people who have gone home and then come in on an elective basis to stay to await surgery (after the need for surgery has been determined) are often better prepared psychologically for the operation. They have time to digest the information the doctor has told them, and they arrive knowing what they want to know—the initial shock of finding out that they have cardiac disease having subsided.

A great deal of personal preparation occurs. Oh sure, the staff can draw the blood work, do the pre-operative prep, teach about the surgery and the post-operative recovery, etc., but truly, the patients themselves are the ones who have to prepare for surgery. A part of that means developing a trust in the team and developing the confidence that everything will go well despite being scared. Those patients who learn that they have severe cardiac disease and then immediately have to stay in hospital to await surgery often have a more difficult adjustment. They are placed, so to speak, on a non-stop roller coaster of emotions and information, and by the end of it all, they recall little of what was said and done prior to the surgery. As a nurse it is important to recognize this and to offer a review of information as often as the patient needs or wants it.

I think, too, one of the most difficult concepts of all for cardiac patients is the total dependence on strangers and the sense of loss of control over themselves. For this reason it is important to enter into a partnership with the health care team— everyone has a role and responsibility, including the patient. It is one thing to be told you have to do something, and quite another to understand what you have to do to get better and then do it. The latter, I feel, is the better way to go. I have found that people do much better when they are given respect and enter into that partnership where they are as responsible for the positive outcome as the rest of the team.

One of the most positive aspects about a cardiac unit is that we are in the business of "fixing broken hearts." We help the people get better. Granted, we can't yet cure heart disease, but, through health prevention education and understanding what causes it, we can slow it down and even stop it from progressing further.

Oh, by-the-way, that first patient I looked after did great. He recovered from his surgery, and although is it was some eight or nine years ago, I still hear from him every now and then. He's had to make many changes in his life style, like giving up smoking and having to eat better, but he feels well and has become a grandfather.

I don't remember all the people I cared for over the years, but each one, in some way, has given me as much as I've given them.

The Angiogram

An angiogram (sometimes called an arteriogram) is a procedure by which a dye is injected into a coronary artery to determine where a narrowing or blockage is occurring and to what extent. A local anesthetic with an intravenous sedation is administered, and you are conscious, although sedated, during this test. A narrow tube (a catheter) is inserted into an artery in the arm or groin area and threaded up towards the heart and into a coronary artery. The physician is guided by a picture on the X-ray screen to perform this task. A radiopaque dye is then injected through the catheter, and a rapid sequence of X-ray photos are taken while this dye travels through the coronary arteries and its branches, letting the cardiologist know where the narrowing or blockage is occurring as well as the severity of it. When the dye is released into the chest, a warm flushing feeling, which is painless, takes place throughout the chest area for a short period. This is the only sensation I felt while undergoing the test.

The catheterization process may also be used to determine the functioning of the valves and walls of the heart. It may be used to diagnose an aneurysm (a bulging of the heart wall or a blood vessel) or a birth defect of the heart, such as a hole in one of the walls between the chambers.

Coronary arteriography (the angiogram) is done in a catheterization laboratory ("cath lab"). I was, as usual when it came to any procedure involving my heart, quite frightened before I underwent this test. When I was having angina pains in the past, I knew at times that I should have had an angiogram to determine the severity of my blockage, but the immediate relief from the chest pains after taking nitro justified, in my mind, not undergoing such a venture. My brother-in-law, John Wilson, had an angiogram, and he told me that there was nothing to it. As well, I had spoken to others who had undergone the procedure and received the same positive endorsement. However, my fear was greater than common sense, and I postponed the inevitable, but now I can tell you that I experienced no pain whatsoever and would not hesitate to undergo this test again if the need arises (although I hope it doesn't).

Here I must say that the presence of a cardiologist with the reassuring temperament of the one who performed my test certainly puts your mind into a relaxed and do-what-you-want-Doc-I-trust-you attitude. As I lay on the table, the cardiologist attempted to insert the catheter into an artery in my groin area. He said, "Burton, I can't find your damn artery; it would have helped me if you had lost some weight." Only an individual such as he could have made this comment and gotten away with it. He made me wish I weighed less just to please him, instead of feeling any resentment towards his remarks.

During the test, you are strapped on a table, and it is rotated at different angles to give you an astronaut-in-space feeling. I was in the Cath Lab to undergo this surgical procedure for approximately one hour. The test usually lasts from 15 minutes to two hours depending on the circumstances. You are admitted to the hospital the day before the test and usually released the day after. Following this procedure, you have to lie on your back for eight hours to give the blood coming out of the artery a chance to coagulate. No stitches are involved, only a piece of adhesive placed over the incision. When the adhesive was removed the following day, I looked at the groin area where all the action had taken place, and it appeared as though someone had been playing darts and had used my groin as the dart board. The cardiologist wasn't kidding about having to probe for that damn artery! Even with this problem, there was no sensation of pain, and if I had not been able to see the puncture marks in my groin area, I would not have believed that they were there.

In the late afternoon after the test, the cardiologist came to the room and gave me the results—three arteries were blocked: one 100%, another 70% and the third 50%. It would be necessary to have coronary bypass surgery. At this instance my mind could not fully comprehend the situation I was about to face. I was not overly upset, but after I had time to mull over what was going to happen to me, I started to experience a feeling of anxiety and fear that controlled my emotions until after surgery. However, my only immediate reaction to the news was to question the doctor: "Will I not be able to have angioplasty instead to remedy this problem?" His reply was an emphatic no. He stated that such a procedure could give me as much chance of dying on the operating table as surviving. These odds did not impress me so, of course, I had no alternative but to agree to a triple bypass. He then stated that Dr. Aldrete would perform the operation and that he would be in to see me later in the evening.

THE ROAD TO A NEW LIFE

The Heart Attack

Frances J. Hintze graduated as a registered nurse in 1953 and then as a midwife in 1954 in England. She worked as a midwife at the British Military Hospital in Berlin, Germany, and then emigrated to Vancouver, British Columbia, with her husband in 1956. There she was a staff nurse, then Assistant Head Nurse in obstetrics and neonatal intensive care.

Due to her husband's work, she relocated to Toronto, and after her divorce in 1978, she was employed full-time as Director of the Neonatal Intensive Care Unit in this city for 12 years. During this period she not only raised two children and assisted them through college, but graduated with a degree in Health Administration herself.

Fran moved to Calgary in December, 1987, where she was a Nurse Clinician in the Special Care Nursery at the Rockyview Hospital. She is presently nursing part-time in the Antepartum Postpartum Unit at this same hospital.

This is Mrs. Hintze's story:

> When Ken asked me to write a chapter for his book, I happily agreed. His story made me realize that we experienced many emotional parallels, yet

there were differences also. If my experience can help others, then this will accomplish its goal.

I was 59 years old when my life was to change quite suddenly one Sunday morning in May. On getting up, I just did not feel well, and I had a tightness in my chest. I put this down to stress—being a newcomer to Calgary and feeling rather lonely; missing my friends in Toronto and changing my job, not without some major difficulties. For the first time in years, I also shared my home with my mother, who is really a wonderful, energetic, intelligent woman. Looking back now, I was not really happy with my life. I smoked at least a pack of cigarettes a day, which did not make me feel good about myself—but I loved to exercise, hike, and particularly play golf.

So off I went this morning with my golf clubs and the intention of picking up a game at a nearby par three course. Surely this would make me feel better. My spirits rose when I got there, and I started out all right but gradually realized that the chest pain did not leave me. I said good-bye to my playing partner and headed back to my car. I then made the best decision of my life—to drive to Rockyview's Emergency Department for a checkup. Although I worked at the hospital, I knew no one in Emergency. When I stated that I suffered from chest pains the nurses moved fast—I found myself hooked up to a monitor and intravenous, and the tests began. A cardiologist happened to be in the building (a real plus on a Sunday afternoon), and since my ECG showed "changes," he decided to admit me and schedule further tests the next day. I was given five nitro pills to keep at my bedside, and if I experienced any further chest pain, I was to call the nurse immediately.

I must admit that at that stage I was not particularly concerned. Only the fact that my family—mother, brother, and his wife, daughter, and her husband and three lovely grandchildren—came to see me at once made me realize that they were worried about me.

At midnight I had a full blown heart attack—occlusion of the right coronary artery! Through the excruciating pain in my chest, my jaw, the pins and needles in both arms, my mind was racing, and I was convinced that I was going to die, so wanted to see my family again. The speed of nursing and medical intervention was overwhelming, and I trustingly gave up control over my body to them. Being a nurse myself did not calm me since my specialty is obstetrical nursing, a field far removed from cardiology, and I could only guess at what was going on. With "miracle" TPA (a blood clot dissolver) and other medication, I pulled through the acute stage, and once I stabilized, there was an emotional moment with my family who had come to see me. For me the best thing that morning was to see my daughter's face. I felt such hope with my family close by, and I secretly vowed to live a healthier lifestyle for their sake.

I remember the first night after my heart attack very distinctly—I could not sleep but relived the previous night's happenings over and over. For many days I felt teary-eyed and depressed. It was hard to see beyond tomorrow. How much damage was there? How much physical activity would I be able to carry on with? My director of nursing sent word that I was not to worry about work or my future at work. This meant the world to me! The nurses, from the first day on, impressed me with their knowledge and encouragement. I submitted

willingly to the barrage of tests and finally an
angioplasty. To date this procedure has been a success.

After 10 days in the hospital, I returned to my
condominium. I recall the next two months as
being emotionally difficult. Everyone seemed to
tell me what to do, in an attempt to protect me. I
should really have said that everyone told me what
NOT to do. I realize now that I must have been difficult to live with.

I was tuned into my chest as though with an
amplifier. Any small pain or heart irregularity
frightened me. The medication gave me
oesophageal spasms, and all in all it was not a
pleasant recovery period. I started to walk but did
not really know how much physical activity was
good for me. Looking back, I was extremely self-
centered, depressed and angry with the loss of control over my life.

The turning point for me was my acceptance
into the cardiac rehabilitation program. I was keen
to start this program and used my professional
connections to get in early. Having a primary
nurse overseeing me during this period helped a
great deal. Her guidance and calm reassurance were
just what I needed. Exercising on the treadmills
and bikes gave me back confidence, and there were
other heart attack victims there—I was not alone.
The courses given on diet and stress are invaluable.
Last but not least, I was contacted by the Heart to
Heart Society, a group of ex-cardiac rehabilitation
graduates who get together once a month. This
group provides education and support for cardiac
patients in need of such services, and as well raises
funds for the cardiac rehab program. It is also a fun
group, and I soon felt that I wanted to give some-

thing in return; hence my involvement with hospital visitation.

My employer generously supported my decision to continue work on a part-time basis in a different unit where the acuity of patients was less severe. I love my work there and enjoy that there are so many opportunities to assist the patients. And my co-workers are wonderful people.

Through "Heart to Heart," I have met people like Ken who make others feel better. In the end, it is people who enrich our lives.

As a person with coronary heart disease, I can say that it takes time to learn to listen to the body. I had to make some lifestyle changes but gained the knowledge that those changes were worthwhile. I hope to live a meaningful life for many years yet.

Thanks to so many wonderful people, family, friends, nurses, doctors, everyone at the cardiac rehab and Heart to Heart, I look with confidence to each new day.

THE BALLOON TREATMENT

Angioplasty

Angioplasty is a nonsurgical treatment designed to open clogged arteries. It is much like the arteriogram or angiogram that was described previously. You are awake while it is being done. When it works, angioplasty opens the artery and restores blood flow. Most people leave the hospital 24 to 48 hours after angioplasty.

Angioplasty is one of the ways of treating buildup in arteries (atheroschlerosis). In this treatment, a catheter with a small balloon on the end is placed in a clogged artery. The balloon is then inflated and deflated several times to try to stretch the artery and flatten the deposits against the wall. If the balloon can flatten them, the artery opens up, and good blood flow returns. For some people, angioplasty replaces the pain and inconvenience of bypass surgery.

Your doctor cannot predict ahead of time if angioplasty will work. Sometimes the buildup is too hard and does not respond to the balloon. Also, trying to open up an artery could lead to total artery blockage. If this happens during coronary angioplasty, immediate bypass surgery may, in some cases, be needed to bring back blood flow and prevent heart damage.

You may be given medication before angioplasty to

help you relax, and you will be awake during the procedure. A needle attached to IV (intravenous) fluids is put in an arm vein. Medications and fluids can be given through this tube.

ECG pads (electrodes) are placed on the arms and/or legs or trunk. These record your heartbeat. Your blood pressure is also checked from time to time.

An introducer sheath (tube) is then put into the artery, usually through the groin area. A catheter is guided through this sheath up to the opening of the narrowed artery. X-ray dye is injected to take a picture of the blocked artery. The dye may cause a "hot" feeling or brief nausea.

As the balloon catheter is being placed in the narrowed artery, you may be asked to cough or take a deep breath. This will help the catheter move into just the right place. This is most helpful in coronary angioplasty since the arteries are small and have many side branches. The doctor may need to use several catheters before one can be moved into the correct position.

When the catheter is in place, the doctor will slowly inflate the balloon. He will closely watch the X-ray view of the artery. For the moment you may have your original symptoms, since the inflated balloon temporarily stops blood flow to the narrowed artery. Even though these symptoms are not surprising, it is important to let the doctor know so the balloon can be deflated or medications given.

After the balloon is deflated, X-ray dye is injected into the narrowed artery to see if the opening inside the artery is bigger. When the artery has been opened as much as possible, the balloon catheter is removed.

For patients having coronary angioplasty, after the balloon catheter is removed, the introducer sheath is usually left in place for 2 to 3 hours. Sometimes the sheath must stay in overnight. The sheath acts as a plug until the blood begins to clot normally.

The total bed rest needed after coronary angioplasty may be eight to nine hours but can last 24 hours, depending partly on when the introducer sheath can be removed.

You are usually discharged from the hospital on the day following angioplasty. Coronary angioplasty began in 1977, and the first patient is still fully active and free of angina symptoms.

As stated previously, I was not a candidate for angioplasty, and therefore cannot personally describe the feeling of going through such a procedure. Here again, I have asked Fran Hintze to help me out, as she did in the previous chapter, where she described her feelings when going through the trauma of a heart attack. She has consented to write about her experience with having angioplasty:

Following an angiogram, my cardiologist advised me to have angioplasty in order to unblock the right coronary artery. I was transferred from the Rockyview Hospital, where I felt rather "at home" since I worked there, to the Holy Cross Hospital in Calgary. I should mention that the former is a bright beautiful facility, whereas the Holy is an older hospital, which, however, enjoys a wonderful medical reputation. Arriving in a small room on the fifth floor, I looked out the window and could see a hill of graves! Was this to be an omen?

I also knew that my son and daughter-in-law were coming in that night from Toronto, and I had to ask permission for them to visit me late—after visiting hours. All this and my fear of the next day's procedure finally overcame me—I sobbed and sobbed uncontrollably, much to the nurses' consternation. It's amazing what a good cry will do for you. After calm returned, I realized that tomorrow would come and go and that, if successful, the artery would be unclogged and my chest pain and health problem would decrease.

The trip to the Angiocath Suite was not new to me—I remembered the angiogram only too well. Strangely enough, knowing what to expect helped relieve my anxiety. I should mention that one of the cardiovascular surgeons breezed by prior to the procedure indicating that in case of `a rupture', he would meet me in the Operating Room, for which he needed formal consent. We agreed that we would rather NOT meet again under similar circumstances. This incident frightened me more than I realized, and I thought about such a thing happening all during the procedure.

I found the angioplasty more interesting than anything else. The cardiologist explained every step of the procedure, and was gentle and confident in handling the sheath and catheter. Lying in one position over a period of hours with a large pressure bandage on my groin was, for me, more unpleasant than the acute pain from needles and tests. I cannot say enough good things about the nursing staff and certainly my physicians. I was monitored carefully, encouraged when I felt down, given a bedpan when I requested it and finally, when there was no danger of bleeding, I was discharged.

I will say that I felt extremely tired and weak going home the morning after angioplasty. I was lucky to have people at home who assisted me to the shower, on my first walk and with my meals.

That no one really told me how much I could safely do made me feel pretty insecure, and at times overcareful. I wondered how far to walk and where I could go. (Driving a car in my case was not permitted for six weeks.) This is where the cardiac rehabilitation program provided answers and gave me back a lot of confidence.

A Valve Job

Bob (Robert Thomas) Sterling and his wife Betty are residents of Shellbrook, Saskatchewan, a small farming community approximately 90 miles northeast of Saskatoon. Bob was born in Shellbrook 70 years ago. When he was 19 years old, he contacted rheumatic fever (a common disease before antibiotics), which caused damage to the aortic valve in his heart, As a result, on July 8, 1991, he underwent open-heart surgery to replace this valve.

Valves are essential to the heart's pumping function. The heart has four valves, or tissue flaps, that open and close like one-way doors, allowing blood to move between the heart's four chambers each time it beats. The aortic valve is one of these valves—the other three are called the mitral valve, the pulmonary valve and the tricuspid valve. The aortic and mitral valves are the ones most often damaged by rheumatic fever, birth defects or infection.

Bob's replacement valve is commonly called a "pig valve (porcine bioprosthesis)." It was my interpretation (with no understanding of heart valves prior to writing this) that the complete valve was taken from a pig and in whole, replaced in a human. It's strange and rather humorous (although certainly not to the pig) to visualize poor old Porky being wheeled in on a table beside the patient, to prepare for the necessary transplant. In my days around the hospital, I never have seen any pigs, waiting to make that ultimate sacrifice to humanity.

There are two general types of artificial valves. One is a mechanical valve made of metal and the other a biological valve made of human or animal tissue, often combined with a supportive artificial skeleton. Most of the biological valves are taken from pigs or made of bovine tissue, giving them the name porcine valves. Scientists have discovered that the valve leaflets of the pig are the closest tissue found that can be substituted for a human's. The great advantage of tissue valves is that "blood thinners" (anticoagulants) that prevent the development of clots around the valves are required for only a short time after the operation in many cases, in contrast to the permanent requirement in the case of mechanical valves. However, mechanical valves of modern design should last almost indefinitely. Porcine valves appear to hold up well for many years, depending on which valve they are replacing and on the techniques of their preservation, but more experience is required for a complete evaluation. A third type of valve is called a homograft. These valves are removed from people who have died of a disease that does not affect the heart.

During a heart-valve replacement operation, you are under a general anesthetic and your circulation and breathing are taken over by a heart-lung machine. An incision is made along your breastbone. Your sternum is parted and your heart is exposed. The beating of the heart is stopped by an infusion of potassium, and any damaged valves are cut out. The new valve or valves are then sewn into place with stitches that will not dissolve once you have healed. The operation takes from two to four hours.

During the summer of 1992, we visited Bob and Betty, during which time I taped Bob's experience with his valve replacement. The following is Bob's account of this procedure:

I had rheumatic fever when I was 19 and spent three months in bed with it. I was pretty hefty when I was young, weighing 195 pounds with a 26 inch waist, but after three months, I was down to 100 pounds.

It started right after New Year's—I got a throat infection that turned into quinsy (a tonsil infection). After about four days, I couldn't get my clothes on, so I hollered for my dad to help me. He got me downstairs, and I never got upstairs again for six months. Dr. Coffyne was called, and when he came out to the farm and realized how serious my sickness was, he ordered a special nurse out of Prince Albert. She came out for about 10 days, until the sickness subsided.

I was so weak that I couldn't stand the covers on me, so dad made a special cage to hold the bed sheets off my body. I sweated so much, they had to change the bed sheets five times in a day.

I came through the experience relatively well, although they told me that I had a heart murmur (a leakage of the heart).

Afterwards I did manage to get into the service—the only one that would accept me was the navy. They said I would never get into the army or the air force.

After the war, I went to Dr. Tucker for a checkup, and, although he was surprised that I got into the service after having rheumatic fever, he couldn't find any trace of the heart murmur or leakage anymore.

I was, however, always short of breath. In the old days at harvest time, after a few days of being out at 6:00 in the morning until 7:00 at night, I usually got into pretty good shape, but I could never get into this condition after my bout with the fever.

This condition went on until a year ago last February, when I bought a new car. I applied for a loan at the bank, and, because of my age, I had to go for a check-up in order to get insurance on the loan.

I didn't see that this would be any problem, so I went to a local doctor, Dr. Fung, who gave me a ECG and then said I should see a specialist, suggesting I go into Prince Albert to see Dr. Walker. Dr. Walker, a specialist in diagnostic and internal medicine, gave me a couple of tests and then asked me to come back in a couple of days for a stress test. The minute this test was completed, he phoned a specialist in Saskatoon, saying he had a man in his office, and he wanted the specialist to verify his diagnosis. He didn't tell me at this time what he had found.

When I went to Saskatoon, an aortogram, ventriculogram and coronary cineangiogram were performed, and then the doctors recommended a valve replacement. When the surgeon, Dr. Mycyk, visited me, he explained the choice between a mechanical and a pig valve for my particular problem. We decided to replace my valve with a pig valve. Dr. Mycyk said that I wouldn't like mechanical valves because I would be on warfarin for the rest of my life, and I knew what warfarin does to rats. (Rats will eat warfarin, causing excessive bleeding and eventually death). "The pig valve will go for 20 years in the aortic position," he said, "and if you need another one, we'll replace it, but you'll have a warning period so that this can be done." (Author's note: Bob and I had a chuckle at this time, when the remark was made that he should keep a pig around the farm in case of emergency.)

Right at this time, the nurses were going on strike, and Dr. Mycyk said that he could not very well set me up for a surgical date until the strike ended. After it was over, Dr. Mycyk's receptionist made an appointment for me, but every time I was ready to go, they would phone and set the date back. This occurred twice and I started to feel the effects of the shortage of breath a little more. I began to think that if I didn't get in pretty soon, I wouldn't get in at all as it would be too late. I phoned the hospital, and asked about the possibility of getting in sooner. They said to go to my local doctor and get the ball rolling from there. I went to Dr. Fung, who called Dr. Walker, and he set up some more tests—I was in about six days later.

I went into the University Hospital in Saskatoon on July 6th, and my operation was scheduled for 9:00 AM on July 8th, 1991. On that morning, the nurse came in and said, "I'm going to give you a pill to help you relax." I didn't know whether to be worried or not. I hadn't been worried up to now, and I didn't have any pain, so I thought if I come out of the operation, I've made it, and if I don't, I won't know a damn thing about it anyway—that's the attitude I went in with.

The pill they gave me made me forget even going into the operating room. The next thing I knew, my wife, Betty, and the nurse were standing there. I was wide awake. The nurse said, "You know, I've been here 10 years, and I've never seen anyone come out of an anesthetic so fast." Most times a person will be groggy, but I was wide awake.

I felt 100% and never did have any pain. The only thing bothered me was that the breathing tube was hooked up a little short and the side of my mouth became a little raw and sore because of this.

The following is Betty's description of what she went through during her husband's valve replacement experience:

It was a shock; it sure wasn't what I expected. I think what bothered me more than anything was that Bob was not getting into get his operation as quickly as I thought he should. I lay in bed at night thinking about it, especially after he'd had a couple of bad days, and I realized something had to happen. We thought that if they didn't operate on Bob in Saskatoon soon, we'd try Calgary.

As for as the operation itself, I truly wasn't worried—I had complete confidence in the doctors and in this day and age, such good facilities are available.

I asked Bob if I should come and see him early on the morning of the operation and he said no, that he would be sedated and probably wouldn't even realize that I was there.

The operation was scheduled for 9:00 AM, and I got there at 10:00. The nurses were exceptionally pleasant, gave me coffee and turned the TV on in the room where I waited. Just before 1:00 PM, the operation was over, so the nurse took me to another room where Bob's surgeon came in. He stated that Bob was breathing normally and at the present time was really in much better shape than either he (the doctor) or myself. I was a little tense because, having worked in a hospital, I understood some of the things that could possibly go wrong.

Shortly after 3:00 PM, Bob became conscious, and he knew I was there. The only time a problem occurred was one night after visiting him. He became agitated when I stated I was leaving for the night, so I stayed until later and this calmed him down.

I thought he came through the operation beautifully and much faster than I anticipated. It's a joy to see him walking now without the shortness of breath he had before his operation.

As could be expected, Bob has been subjected to a number of jokes about having a pig valve in him—even his daughters got into the act when they sent him a birthday card with some pigs saying "Oink! Oink!" on it. Because of his disposition, Bob takes these jokes with a grain of salt and even has a chuckle from them himself.

Bob and Betty are very good friends of ours. We saw him after his operation in August, 1991, only one month later. We were vacationing in Waskesiu, a beautiful summer resort in Northern Saskatchewan, when they visited us. It is only now, as I write this, that I realize the incredible short period that had elapsed since he had his operation, and how extremely agile he was at the time, to make such a trip. Most individuals at this time are just attempting a first trip a few blocks to a shopping mall. His stamina is unbelievable.

They have five children (three girls and two boys) and Bob continues (at age 70) to work as a school bus contractor in Shellbrook, while Betty not only has her own business, but also helps out a friend in a local women's fashion store—an amazing and delightful couple!

Bob approached Dr. Mycyk at the University Hospital in Saskatoon for approval to use his name in this story. Dr. Mycyk took the time to authenticate the medical data, phone Bob in Shellbrook and mail an edited chapter back to him. Here again is an example of the type of person I have had the privilege of being exposed to since I started writing this book. Even though I have never met Dr. Mycyk, I hope to have the pleasure to do so some day in the very near future, and thank him personally.

DEPRESSION

PRE OP

"Hi, Mr. Burton—the operation's over and everything went just fine!" This soft-spoken and pleasant voice came out of nowhere.

Were these words coming from one of God's angels or someone in this world? Actually they were spoken by the nurse in ICU who was monitoring my return to reality, although it didn't really matter to me at this time—all my body wanted to do was to go back to the sedated peacefulness of no pain and pleasant rest. I dozed off, and at this juncture had no further memories of this emotional event.

When I visit the cardiac unit at the Holy Cross Hospital, the head nurse gives me a list of patients with the notation "pre op" or "post op" after each name, which simply means that the patient is waiting to be operated on or has already had the operation. Pre ops, of course, fear the unknown, and the majority of those who have been through this trying experience can sense this feeling of apprehension in most patients, while a limited few state that the upcoming ordeal does not affect them at all. I feel that some of this minority actually do have concerns but are not the type to display their emotions, while others have rationalized the pros and cons of the operation and have come to realize that this is the only course to take.

Post ops are through the stage that most of us dreaded (the operation), and are looking forward to a new life. The majority of this group are interested in what's after surgery. This is an exceptionally emotional time for these individuals, and a lot of them seem to grasp at any positive signs to renew their everyday activities—Heart to Heart and Cardiac Rehabilitation are two organizations that can give these patients a positive attitude while returning to everyday tasks.

At this time, it is imperative that patients be told to get on with life after surgery. They must understand the need to start walking, and the drawbacks of sitting around and becoming a couch potato. When I attend Heart to Heart meetings and see the positive attitude of most people (a lot of them older than I), I then try to get this message across to post ops, particularly to those who are "down." As stated before, this whole procedure is about 90% mental and 10% physical—and hopefully, for their own benefit, most cardiac rehabs can develop a positive attitude.

Don't get me wrong; life is more difficult after going through this experience, and I had my downers, but overall, I feel that keeping the mind active and in a positive mood will stimulate the body's recovery and prolong your life.

Although the very last thing I want to do is be pessimistic to anyone who is unfortunate enough to have had a cardiac-related experience, I do feel that it is extremely important to relay the message that there is that remote possibility (as there is with any operation) of not surviving. With many (as in my case) this probability takes control of your emotions and creates a feeling of apprehension and fear, not only for you yourself, but in most instances, also for your family.

My doctor told me that the odds of surviving such an operation were 98% in my favor, and I tried to convince myself that these odds were exceptionally good. But as I said, there was always that 2%, and my mind seemed focused on that psychological fear that takes away all logic. It must have been really traumatic some 30 years ago, when the chances of pulling through such an operation were less than 50%. There are many times when I think back to when my father and oldest brother died, and they didn't even have the availability of a bypass—even 50% odds would have been a blessing at that time.

Heart disease and stroke are Canada's number one killer! It is likely that heart disease or stroke will kill someone you know. Forty-three percent of Canadians who die do so because of this killer. Obviously, we should be concerned.

One of the most unfortunate factors that increase fatalities in this field is that there are not enough medical facilities to handle cardiac and stroke patients in Canada, due to tight hospital budgets, soaring costs and a shortage of highly trained nurses. In the February 13, 1989, issue of *Maclean's* magazine, an article documents one cardiac patient who, having to go through a coronary bypass, had his operation postponed 11 times because of a shortage of beds in the hospital's intensive care unit. As this man waited for his operation, members of his family stated that he appeared to lose his will to live. Even though he finally did have the operation, he died eight days later. His wife and four children were grief-stricken, but said they were not surprised. His wife said that he just went to pieces—he was a broken man.

Ever since I was exposed to cardiac disease, I became more aware of various occurrences and statistics, some of which I have just reviewed. In my personal exposure to heart problems, pre op started for me back in 1976, 16 years ago, although I did not realize it at the time. I was working for Hudson's Bay Oil and Gas and living in Edson, Alberta. One Saturday, we went to Hinton, a town about 55 miles away and, we were shopping at the Bay, one of the few buildings with more than one story in the town. I had walked down to the basement and looked around and then went up to the main floor when I suddenly experienced a sensation of pain in my chest area. I sat down and eventually Marion and the kids caught up to me. The look on my face prompted her remark, "Are you okay?" I replied that I had a slight pain in the chest but said it was probably from something I ate. As she was aware of my family history of heart problems, she wanted me to see a doctor, but like so many of us who initially go through this experience, I put it off by saying it wasn't that big a deal.

During the following years, although I continued to have pains in the chest area, they did not seem to be severe enough to cause me undo alarm, or, as is more likely, I went into that common stage of denial. My mind would not acknowledge that something was wrong with my heart, yet my body was crying out with a message. Luckily, my body remained strong enough to prevent a heart attack, in spite of my mental rejection to its plea for assistance. Sometime in the late 70s, the pain did become severe enough that I saw a doctor about it. I went to see Dr. Singh, who diagnosed angina, and I had my introduction to nitroglycerin pills. Nitro, as it is called, is a tablet placed under the tongue and gives rapid, although temporary, relief from angina. The tongue is chosen because it has a large number of blood vessels that spread the absorption of the medication into your system. Nitroglycerin causes the body's veins and arteries to widen, thus lowering the blood pressure while increasing the flow of blood to the heart. Nitro has, during later years, become available as a spray, which is directed into the mouth, and an ointment that can also be used. A measured amount, as determined by your doctor, is applied to a sealed dressing and placed on the chest or arm. During my visit to Dr. Singh, I became emotionally distraught, and my thoughts immediately turned to dying, and leaving Marion and the kids on their own. At this time Dr. Singh, a complete stranger to me, reacted and consoled me in a manner that I shall never forget. He had that concerned and communicative approach that I look for in medical professionals. When I have a medical problem, I feel much more at ease when treated in this manner. As I stated on page 45, he is a specialist in internal medicine, and I never did see him after my initial visit, although if I had a problem in his field of medicine, I would want to have him as my doctor.

I came home that evening, and Marion immediately knew something was wrong, again I imagine by the expression on my face. Knowing the results of angina pains in my family, I thought it was only a matter of time before I keeled over and had that fatal heart attack. I told her the results of my visit through tears, and the following days were filled with apprehension.

However, as the saying goes, time heals all wounds, and it was only a matter of time that, when nothing out of the ordinary happened, I learned to live with the pain and took a nitro whenever one was warranted. One of the side effects of the pill is that it produces a violent headache in some patients, but only for a short period time. The reason for this is that when nitro expands the arteries and veins it increases the flow of blood not only to the heart, but also to the brain.

In the early 1980s, I did consult with a cardiologist and went through the experience described in "Psychologically Speaking: How Are You Feeling?" The doctor placed me on a treadmill and even after I complained of an uncomfortably severe pain, requested I stay put. Even I knew I had angina, and I finally told him I refused to go any further with the test. Looking back to this exposure, it is my opinion that I probably should have had an angiogram at this time, but this doctor didn't recommend one.

It was not until October, 1989, that the years of living

with and enduring angina pectoris finally caught up to me. During the latter part of the month, it became extremely cold. When going to work, even though I was parked less than a block from the office, I would walk about half way when the pain in my chest became so severe that I would have to go into a building, warm up and pop a nitro. Then, upon reaching the office, I'd take another. This of course started my day with a violent headache, plus the anxiety of wondering how long it would be until that inevitable day when a heart attack would make me another statistic. I think the only thing that saved me from this fate was that I had taken an aspirin every day for the past 10 to 12 years. I had read in a book years ago that aspirin was found to be a blood thinner, and it suggested that taking one a day prevented heart attacks. I thought an aspirin a day wasn't going to hurt me anyway, and the results seemed to cure my problems for a time. These results were new at the time, a fact of which few were aware. Of course, now it is common knowledge, and my cardiologist prescribed it after my operation. When I asked him how long he recommended I take this, he stated for the rest of my life.

One of the side effects of aspirin is that it can cause bleeding in the stomach. Although I have never experienced this problem, the doctor recommended that I take entrophen (a coated aspirin), which does not dissolve in the upper part of the stomach, and this lessens the problem. In any event, any such medication should be cleared through a physician. The one thing I do not intend to do is recommend any cure-all for any illness described in this book. This is one of the things that is essentially important when visiting heart patients as a member of the Heart to Heart Support Society. Even though people mean well by volunteering such information, it could be extremely dangerous because different people react in different ways to medication.

On November 2, 1989, I had an appointment with a cardiologist. I told my supervisor at work that I would be in after I had seen the doctor. Little did I know at that time that I would never again return to work. After the doctor took an ECG and examined me, he said, "You're not going back to work, but into the hospital for an angiogram. In the meantime, I want you at home with complete rest and don't do ANYTHING." The following week, I was admitted to the Holy Cross Hospital and underwent this test, the details of which are described on pages 52 to 54, "The Angiogram."

After I left the hospital, the most helpless feeling I had ever experienced came over me. I became exceptionally emotional and remained so throughout the two-month wait for my operation. I tried my best, and for the most part, I think I succeeded in trying to hide my feelings from the children. I could not hide them from Marion, however, as she stayed pretty close to me during this period, in the event of a heart attack. The waiting period no doubt wore on her nerves, as I know I was not the easiest person to live with at this time. However, on Christmas Day, which is also my birthday, thoughts raced through my mind that this could be my last Christmas with the family, and all the pent-up emotion I had held in came out. I started to cry. I was more concerned then about the scene I had created in front of my children than I was about the upcoming operation. However, as Fran Hintze said in her story on pages 60 to 63, "It's amazing what a good cry will do for you." I did not feel overly distraught again until the day before the operation.

Dr. Aldrete's receptionist instructed me to stop taking aspirin two weeks before the operation. This is so the thinning of the blood caused by this medication is halted, and the blood has a chance to coagulate (thicken) after the operation. Otherwise, a person could bleed to death.

There were things to do that I should have done years

ago, but were put off time and time again. I finally got around to making out a will, as well as listing information on the mortgage, bank accounts, bills payable and all those other household procedures with which Marion was not familiar, so that she, if need be, could carry on without me. As an accountant, I had always handled our financial affairs, and Marion was content with this procedure.

I was admitted to the Holy Cross Hospital on December 31, 1989. The longest and worst day of my life began the next day, New Year's Day, 1990. The thought of the operation scheduled for the next day took over my emotions completely. The scenario was the same as Larry King had written in his book—it was comparable to a condemned man on death's row waiting for that ultimate final moment. I took nitro after nitro during the day, yet the pain in my chest would not go away. George Cairns, one of my roommates, said after the operation that he didn't think I was going to make it through the day as I was an ashen grey and looked as though I was ready to die.

I finally made it through the night. About 6:00 AM the next day the nurse gave me either a pill or an injection (I don't remember which) to sedate me. I think about 8:00 AM they wheeled me out of the room, and I remembered nothing further until awakening from surgery about 5:00 PM.

Open-Heart Surgery

In an April 15, 1990, section of the *Calgary Herald,* there is an article called "A Second Chance," which goes through the procedure used during open-heart surgery at the Foothills Hospital in Calgary. Dr. Kieser, who is on the cardiovascular surgery team at the Foothills, gave permission to Brian Brennan, a writer, and Tom Walker, a photographer, both from the Herald, to be present in the operating room during this surgery. This is a beautifully written article, and I had hoped that I could include it in this book, so I approached Steve Roberts, Assistant Managing Editor at the Herald, to obtain permission. He recommended that this book should be my work (as well as those who have contributed their written articles) and would not have the same projection by using a printed newspaper article, which were the efforts of someone else. I could see where he was coming from, and agreed with his remarks. A person could go through article after article that was already printed, and make a book of these stories, but it would seem that there is no accomplishment by the author and little interest to the reader, particularly if the reader had read the article somewhere else. I am certain there would also be repercussions from the authors of these articles.

I thank those who helped at the *Calgary Herald,* and a special thanks to Brian Brennan. Brian's helpful suggestions assisted me along that path a novice hope-to-be-author must travel, easing my journey considerably.

I do not remember any of the details while undergoing surgery. Thank goodness! I have used some of the terminology in "A Second Chance," as Steve Roberts recommended, and have referred to various medical publications.

I first met Dr. Victor Aldrete, a cardiovascular and thoracic surgeon, about 7:00 PM on November 8, 1989, the day I had my angiogram. When he walked into the room, he projected a self-confidence that instilled trust. His relaxed yet positive approach initiated an immediate liking to him, and that such a reassuring characteristic helped me cannot be overemphasized. I was, after all, a person facing the most traumatic experience in his life, and I was placing this life in the hands of a complete stranger.

Dr. Aldrete went through a complete analysis of the bypass operation, explaining how a vein would be removed from my leg and connected to the aorta at unclogged points in the artery beyond the obstruction, and if required, the mammary artery would be grafted in the same manner. This would alter the flow of blood to the heart (similar to a stream being diverted when a new channel is dug and the old one is blocked) and alleviate the pain experienced when the blood attempted to flow through the partially blocked arteries.

He compared the arteries around the heart to the piping in a sink. If these pipes are plugged, you first put draino or some other deplugging agent down the pipes to clear the obstruction. With the heart, you first try medication, and this will either:

1. with the help of nitroglycerin, expand the arteries to relieve the flow or

2. reduce the heart rate or lower the blood pressure with the help of a beta-blocker or calcium antagonists. These also reduce the likelihood of dangerous heart irregularities (arrhythmia).

The doctor referred to himself as the plumber who was going to repair my clogged sink. Dr. Aldrete concluded his visit leaving me much more informed about what was in store for me. I was to contact his office for a further medical and to arrange a date for surgery.

Shortly after I contacted Dr. Aldrete's office, his receptionist called me back and asked if I would like to be operated on just before Christmas or just after. I immediately speculated that if I were going to depart this world during my operation, I might as well have one last Christmas at home, so settled on a January 2, 1990, date. I considered myself very fortunate to be able to have surgery so soon, as countless individuals across Canada must wait longer for operations and, in some cases, will die before they are operated on.

As I was scheduled for the first operation in the New Year at the Holy Cross Hospital, I halfheartedly joked that I hoped the doctors and nurses hadn't partied too much over the holiday, so they wouldn't approach my operation with massive hangovers.

About 6:00 on the morning of the operation, I was given either a pill or a needle to sedate me, I don't remember which. I don't know if I received any further medication for this purpose through the IV in my arm, but I do know I don't remember leaving my room, or even where the operating room was in the Holy Cross Hospital. I have read and heard that the anesthetists have told patients that they were going to do certain things to them before putting them to sleep, but if anything was done to me, I don't remember.

Two cardiovascular surgeons are in attendance during heart surgery. In addition, seven others assist in the operation—two anesthetists, two perfusionists (who operate the artificial heart-lung pump), a scrub nurse (who looks after the surgical instruments) and two circulating nurses (who perform any other necessary chores, such as obtaining additional supplies such as instruments, drugs, blood or any other item required). I asked Dr. Aldrete after my operation who assisted him and was told it was Dr. Stan Goldstein. I never did learn the names of any of the others. The first surgeon makes an incision down the centre of the patient's chest. The breastbone is sliced with an oscillating power saw and then separated with a stainless steel retractor. The heart is then exposed by opening the pericardium (a sac in which the heart lies).

Simultaneously, the second surgeon makes one or several incisions in the leg, and a length of vein is removed.

Before any incisions are made in the coronary arteries, the patient is connected to a heart-lung machine. This takes over the function of the heart and lungs while the surgeon repairs the heart.

A section of the vein taken from the leg is then sewn to a coronary artery in a point below the blockage. If several arteries are blocked, they can be bypassed by using other sections from the same leg vein, or an arterial graft can be taken from the chest (the internal mammary artery).

During surgery, a lot of equipment is used to watch your body and assist your breathing, measure the pressure and function of your heart, check your blood pressure, follow your heart rate, drain fluids from your body and monitor the workings of your kidneys.

After surgery, you will still be connected to much of the equipment. This does not mean that things are not going well—the equipment simply checks how your body is working.

Some of the equipment includes a breathing (endotracheal) tube, which goes through your mouth and into your windpipe, and is connected to a machine called a ventilator that breathes for you during and after surgery, until you build up enough strength to breath without it; a Swan-Ganz catheter placed in a neck vein measures the pressures in your heart; IVs (intravenous) put in your veins let you receive fluid and medication; an arterial line placed in a wrist artery checks your blood pressure and draws blood samples without continuously giving needles for this purpose; chest drainage tubes placed in the chest drain the blood and fluid that collects in the chest after surgery; a heart monitor connected to your chest by sticky pads (electrodes) records your heart rate and rhythm; a bladder catheter is a small tube put in the bladder to collect urine; and a temporary pacemaker (a small box that is outside the body and connected to the heart with two wires) lets your doctor change your heart rate as needed. When recovering after surgery, these two wires are left sticking out of your chest for a period of five to seven days. We referred to these as our starter or jumper cables.

The heart-lung machine is then disconnected, allowing blood to flow back into the heart and the coronary arteries.

Finally, the breast bone is wired together, and the chest is sewn up.

I had no feeling of any sensations during my operation. After the surgery, I woke up in ICU, still sedated and all I wanted to do was sleep. I had no feeling of pain or discomfort whatsoever.

It was only after being moved from ICU two days after the operation that I had any concerns. I kept bugging the nurse about the bladder catheter and asked her if it was going to hurt when it was removed. My consistent apprehension on this subject finally brought this remark from my nurse: "Oh, you men, all you can worry about are your crown jewels. I'm going to take that tube out of there right now, and it's not going to hurt you one bit."

She went and got the necessary materials (antiseptic, etc.) and removed the tube. As she stated, I experienced no pain and was thankful to be rid of a piece of equipment that was a constant a source of agitation, even though it caused me no discomfort.

As I stated earlier, with the exception of the two cardiovascular surgeons, the other medical personnel involved in this operation are unknown to me. When I think of the role they play in prolonging a life placed in their hands, I only wish there were some way that these persons could be more recognized for their devotion to humanity and the medical profession. The feeling of gratitude for these individuals cannot be expressed in words, and I am certain that the majority of patients going through this operation experience this same gratitude.

To all of you, who assisted during my operation, my heartfelt (no pun intended) thanks for your contribution to my successful coronary bypass surgery.

I See You
(24 Hours a Day)

Anyone familiar with an Intensive Care Unit (ICU) knows that the patients in this area are under 24 hour surveillance to ensure that the critical time in their illness is constantly monitored.

My stay in ICU at the Holy Cross Hospital after open-heart surgery was short (two days), and I won't say sweet, but it was uneventful. I make this statement because I don't remember 90% of my stay there, and during the other 10%, I was in a stupor and didn't really care what happened. This is the place I entered, unconscious, with ten tubes in my body and left with my senses regained and with only one tube left (the bladder catheter).

Since I was operated on, I have heard time and time again people making frightening comments about the tubes used during and after an operation. The disheartening part of this situation is, that in many cases, the people passing on these comments have never gone through this experience, and really don't know what they are talking about. There is an example of this on page 129, "Peter and Dem: Different Patients, Different Feelings," where the woman visiting was making unsavory remarks about open-heart surgery, yet had never been through the operation herself. The one tube in particular that comes up most in conversations is the breathing (endotracheal) tube, which goes through your mouth and into your windpipe. I can assure you that *in my experience* I remember very little about this time and to this day do not recall any discomfort from any tube I had in my body. I was apprehensive with the one tube they did leave in me (the bladder catheter), and the only reason for this was that by the time it had to come out, I was out of ICU and no longer under the strong sedation that dulled my feelings. Actually, there was no reason to have any uneasiness about this tube whatsoever. Other people may have different reactions to this tube situation. I know that if I ever go through a similar operation, I would discuss sedation with my surgeon, and the strength used to alleviate apprehension. As I had stated, I was a potential basket case before I was operated on, and this may have resulted in instructions to the nurses that sedation with me be stronger than with some others. I honestly don't know—I just do know that whatever sedation I did receive, it kept me calm and relaxed.

One comment the nurse in ICU did make was that the strength of my sedation was being decreased gradually. This is done so that you become more conscious and capable of strengthening your breathing capabilities, and so you don't become too dependent on the ventilator. The sooner you begin to breathe at a determined strength, the sooner the endotracheal tube is removed. This, I understand, is why you should try to accept this procedure and assist yourself back to normal breathing.

The staff in ICU have consented to compile a short documentary on their section. The following are their comments.

Patients from ICU are often at the most vulnerable period in their lives, both emotionally and physically. Their families are also under a lot of stress at this time.

Patients' initial contact with ICU is often when they are first diagnosed with cardiac disease. They and their families are quickly subjected to the implications of the diagnosis, and its threat to their life and emotional well-being.

The post open-heart surgical patient is also extremely vulnerable. All control of physical care is handed over to the expertise of nurses and skilled technicians. The patients and their loved ones become dependent on strangers. It is often a frightening time, a time when a great deal of emotional support is needed on top of the physical care given. Happily, the nurses in ICU have the necessary skills, caring attitude and access to a multi-disciplinary team to provide this support.

Many people affect the care a patient receives in ICU. The nurse coordinates this team, ensuring that proper resources are mobilized. The nurse's role is concentrated in the physical and technical areas, but she or he can see the person under the tubes and machines, and provides support to patients and their families as they move through the stages of illness. Other team members are called in as necessary.

Patients can rest assured that their fears and needs are understood and responded to. They are very much partners in the care they receive. Gradually, during their stay in ICU, they are given greater control of their care and the knowledge required to carry it out. Families are encouraged to take part in this process as well, so that a frightening experience can become a learning experience.

ELATION

Post Op

After my operation, coming back to reality was really an uneventful occasion. It was somewhere around 5:00 PM, I was later informed, and I wasn't aware of my surroundings. With the exception of realizing I had made it through the operation, I had no other thoughts. I did say a prayer to God and thanked Him, although I don't remember when this took place. I also developed a strong feeling of wanting to pass my experience on to others, and here again, I don't know when this occurred. I do know it was during my stay in ICU. I compared myself to someone spreading the gospel, and it seemed like I wanted to go out and preach to everyone saying "Don't worry if you have to undergo open-heart surgery. It's more than possible you won't remember what happened to you during the critical stage anyway."

After I left the hospital, and later joined the Heart to Heart Support Society, I visited a limited number of those yet to go through surgery. I then realized that countless others were not receiving any assistance after they left the hospital, and my thoughts turned to writing a book. In many of the smaller areas, facilities are not available to seek help, and I am not aware if similar societies have been formed in other urban centers. But even though discharged heart patients may receive help from others in this manner, my hope is that this book will deliver a further message of hope.

On Thursday about noon, my stay in ICU drew to a close, and I was moved into a semi-private room. I wanted to return to a ward but at the time they were full. The nurse said that a patient was being discharged from one the next morning, and they would transfer me to a ward then. She also asked if I could give some support to the patient in the room to which I was going. Even at this early period after my operation, the nurses must have detected my optimistic outlook and wanted me to try to pass some of this optimism on to my roommate in an attempt to pacify him. This individual was in the same shape I was before my operation, frightened and uncertain of the future. It did not help that his wife had open-heart surgery eight years before, and she constantly reminded him of the terrible ordeal she had experienced with the tube down her throat. Even though procedures had advanced immeasurably during this time, this poor soul was being subjected to a conversation that continuously increased his anxiety.

One of the disturbing events I witnessed was that the family was continuously praying, and each time they said a prayer, it seemed to drive the patient into a deeper depression. It almost appeared as though they thought he were not going to return from his operation, and they were going to make certain that he was ready to meet his Maker. I am a God-fearing person, and while the possibility of dying exists, I do feel that a patient doesn't need to be constantly reminded of it. After all, the possibility of surviving is much greater, and a pessimistic attitude only puts the patient into the emotional trauma that I went through and found unwarranted.

However, I did have private moments with my companion. I know the talks we had during this time alleviated a lot of the tension he was under. I am certain he approached the operation with a much better attitude, than if we had never met. During his recovery, he confirmed this and thanked me for the words of reassurance I had given him during our one-on-one chats.

I experienced a pleasant incident during my short stay in this room. I got to meet the minister whom the family had called in, the Rev. Gerald E. Graham, and I developed an instant liking for him. He had been in the air force for many years, which created a common bond between us. He was the type of minister that I could go to church and listen to without that urge to constantly glance at my watch, wishing the sermon were over. We had lunch together some months later. I would have enjoyed going to his church, but unfortunately, he had just reached 65 and retirement. I was shocked to pick up the paper a year later to discover his name in the obituaries on May 21, 1991. Gerry looked the picture of health the last time I saw him. He did not have that long to enjoy his retirement but was certainly more prepared than most of us to meet his Boss.

Thursday evening, Marion, Barb and Doug came to see me. They were surprised to find me sitting up. The nurse came into the room, and when she asked me to go for a walk, I thought all three of their mouths would hit the floor. I walked slowly with the nurse, my son and my daughter, down the hall. The nurse said we would go to the nurses' station (halfway down the hall) and return. I said "Why don't we walk to the end of the hall and back." She did not have to respond because by that time we had reached our stipulated designation, I was so tired I had to rest. I was then quite content to return to my room.

After a heart operation, patients are very tender in the chest area, and their Teddy is never out of reach. If you visit a cardiac ward and see a patient walking around clutching what looks like a pillow to his chest, don't think he's lost his marbles. The Teddy is a towel wrapped in a pillowcase and post-ops clutch this to their breasts to relieve the pain felt when they have to cough, take a deep breath, or just when there is a sudden movement like getting in and out of bed and ironically, sometimes to laugh.

While you are recuperating, you will constantly have hospital personnel attempting to bring your body back to the state it was originally in. At times, some patients are irritated by the requests made, but here I emphasize that it is extremely important to cooperate with these professionals. They are trying to make you better. Any help you give them to make their task easier only helps your recovery.

One of the duties you will be asked to perform is to blow into a machine called an incentive respirometer. This is a plastic box with a ball in it that goes up a plastic tube as you blow and measures the pressure you exert. It seems a very simple thing to do, but unfortunately, those of us who have had our chest opened find it difficult to perform this rehabilitation procedure as it puts pressure on the chest and in plain language—it hurts. As you continue to go through this procedure, it gets easier and easier, the ball goes higher and higher, and of course your lungs get stronger and stronger. I considered it a challenge and was not going to let some little plastic container get the better of me. As a result, I soon became proficient at putting that old ball up the tube to the desired measurement. This, of course, made me that much stronger that much sooner.

After your operation, you are a chartered member of the zipper club as your chest looks as though it could be zippered open and shut if desired. Your leg, though not visible to many, is the same. One thing that I found different since my last operation requiring stitches (16 years old with appendicitis) was that steel staples were now used for stitching. Although this procedure was new to me, I could see the advantage when they were removed. They came out much easier and did not have that pulling through the skin, as with the old method.

At some point after surgery, you realize there are two wires sticking out of you in the heart area. As mentioned earlier, we referred to these as our starter or jumper cables. They allow doctors to administer an instant jolt of electricity if such a need is required. The only problem I had with these was that the area where they came out of my body would not heal, and the nurses were constantly changing dressings. After about four days in the ward, Dr. Aldrete pulled these out, and I had no further problem. When he did pull out the wires, I felt an instant jolt in the heart, and I knew that the wires had been there.

Over the days, activities in our ward developed into a routine, and the four of us developed a bond that cannot be explained to those who are not subjected to this experience. Each morning, as we got our 2:00 AM awakening, we would chat after the nurses left. Time was not a factor in our lives, as we could sleep anytime, and this seemed to be a period to express comments that were not said when we had visitors. I am sure glad that some of our conversations were not taped. One of the patients mentioned at this time that it sure itched down inside his chest. I replied, "That's a good sign; it means that you're healing. Just open your mouth, stick your hand down your throat and scratch yourself." My roommate replied, *"That's* what the problem is. I've been trying to reach it from the other end and have had no success."* Of course, this brought out gales of laughter, and you'd think we were having a party instead of trying to recuperate from the most serious operation of our lives. The expression "It only hurts when you laugh" certainly applied to us, as each time we laughed it hurt, even though it was next to impossible to contain this laughter.

I recall receiving only one needle (I could have had a blood test or two but don't remember) while recovering. This was a daily injection of heparin in the stomach. Heparin is a blood thinner, and keeps the blood from developing a clot in the leg veins after the operation. I got this needle for about five days after I came out of ICU, and this procedure was not at all painful. It hurt less than a blood test.

On Friday, only three days after my surgery, one of my buddies visited and we had a game of gin rummy (I won five dollars). I began to fall back into that established routine I had before coming to the hospital, and after a few more days, I had the urge to go home.

George Cairns left the hospital two days before I did. No sooner was he out of the room than his bed was taken by a new patient. This chap was a new Canadian who had emigrated from Europe. He had much the same "what's going to happen to me" look that is so predominant in those awaiting surgery. His biggest concern was that he wanted a private room and kept asking the nurse for one. She finally became agitated and told him that no such rooms were available, and if there were, he didn't need one and was quite fine where he was.

My initial reaction to this fellow roommate was that he thought he was too good to share a room with us. Actually, after we got talking, I gathered that because of his customs, he probably felt more comfortable without having to share this emotional part of his life with people of a different race and culture.

After a few hours in the company of his three companions, a relaxed atmosphere began taking over his emotions, and he had numerous queries about what was going to happen to him. With the positive response he got from the three of us, I think at this time, if a nurse came in and told him that there was a private room available for him, he would have turned it down. I still visit this person from time to time, and enjoy my association with him very much.

The following Thursday, nine days after my operation, I was discharged. The day before, half my stitches were removed, and on Thursday morning, the rest came out. This procedure also was not painful.

After I had gotten out of bed in the hospital and became a little more active, I was constantly chatting with those about to go through what I had just experienced. I feel the optimistic message I tried to convey to these people was there, and I am certain that I didn't make anyone more apprehensive. Larry Kwong (the owner of Foodvale in Calgary) was one patient who came in and was as frightened as I was, if not more so. Larry was slated to have a single or a double bypass, but when they opened him up, this increased to six (a sextuple), and he almost didn't make it. He was extremely distraught before his operation, and I dropped in on him as much as possible to try and alleviate his fears. I gave him Larry King's book *Mr. King, You're Having a Heart Attack,* I anticipating that it would do the same for him as it did for me. He was to be operated on the day before I was discharged, and I talked to him before he went for surgery. I asked him if the book had helped and when he said it had, I felt I had accomplished something. Just lately, I dropped in to see Larry, telling him I was writing a book and was curious to know to what extent reading Mr. King's book had helped him. He confessed to me then (2 1/2 years after the operation) that he could not read the book as it terrified him to get involved in anything to do with the operation. He was such a gentleman that he did not want to offend me at the time we were in the hospital. His reaction was the same as the one Miss Stewart talks about on page 49, "We Fix Broken Hearts: The Cardiac Unit." Here she states that her first patient did not want to know anything about the operation. She found this a strange request, but respected his wishes, and after she became more familiar with heart patients, she could see why some want this type of treatment.

Thursday morning, as I was getting ready to leave the hospital, I discovered Mrs. Kwong in the hallway with tears in her eyes. I almost hated to approach her, as I thought the worst. During the previous evening, Larry's condition had deteriorated rapidly, but through the skill of Dr. Aldrete (he performed Larry's operation as well as mine), who had to operate again during the night, Larry survived. Today Larry looks and feels as healthy as I do, and he really enjoys that game of golf that would have been an impossibility if it hadn't been for open-heart surgery.

Many people go through a post-depression period after surgery. A lot feel helpless, like they will never be able to return to a normal life. Some individuals never do get over this attitude, but they are their own worst enemy. Here once again, the 10% physical 90% mental ratio comes into play. I was so pleased to pull through the operation that I never really succumbed to depression. Before leaving the hospital, a person is given numerous verbal instructions about how to carry on in life, and booklets are supplied for constant reference. The cardiac rehabilitation program also contributes a great deal to the emotional, as well as the physical, rehabilitation of heart patients.

I will try to provide answers to some of the most-asked questions that both patients and their relatives have about returning home. You usually start driving about four to six weeks after discharge. You should start walking short distances at first (one-half block), which will be gradually increased. If you get tired, stop and rest—your body will dictate the level of activity you should attempt. Be extremely careful that you do not slip on a scatter rug or some similar object around the house, and if you are walking outside, watch for slippery patches. Do not lift more that five to ten pounds for four to six weeks after surgery. Don't do anything that will put pressure on your chest during this period, like opening stuck windows, prying open a jar, moving furniture or opening and closing heavy doors. Because the sternum takes a full six months to a year to completely close, very heavy lifting (i.e. furniture, appliances) should be avoided until then. Ease into recreation by playing cards, practice putting instead of playing golf, go to the theater, paint pictures, go to spectator sports where there are no large crowds, and take part in other similar activities. Smoking is the worst thing you can do to your heart—JUST DON'T!

Participating in sexual activity may also cause you some concern. Not only might you worry about sex after surgery, but so might your partner. Your body will dictate what action you should take—just don't put pressure on your chest. If you are tired or tense, wait until you are relaxed. If you feel at all uneasy, allow more time for hugging and caressing. Most doctors advise a woman not to have a baby for at least a year after surgery. Some contraceptives can be harmful to heart patients. Check with the hospital before leaving if you are concerned about sexual activity or birth control.

There are also some restrictions regarding alcohol. If you do not have an addiction, you can drink two ounces of whiskey, or seven ounces of wine, or 17 ounces of beer in one day. Too much alcohol is known to weaken the heart muscles. Don't over-tire yourself by having too many visitors. Let your body dictate your activity. It will tell you when you are tired and if you are—rest.

Finally, I would like to say that we who live in Calgary, and have heart problems, are very fortunate to have not only the top heart-team professionals in the world at our doorstep, but the cardiac rehabilitation program at the General Hospital, which is the most impressive program I have ever been fortunate enough to be involved in.

If you are in the Calgary area, and do have the opportunity to go through this program after your heart problem, DON'T TURN IT DOWN! It will not only bring you back to a normal lifestyle, but it will give you that morale boost that is so essential at this time in your life.

Emotional Effects on the Family

Someone hit by a sudden heart attack or some other cardiac illness often develops a feeling of frustration, helplessness and/or hostility. These reactions are often spontaneous and do not make this individual the easiest person to get along with. Unfortunately, these emotions affect family and friends.

I have a family who gave me support even though they were subjected to these feelings. Their comments, while going through a trying period with my cardiac illness, are documented here.

MARION

I do not relish the memory of my husband's transfer to Edson in January of 1976. It was a cold, bitter day in Calgary, and with the doors open for the movers, it got very chilly in the house. The movers were late arriving, and so it was very late in the evening before they finished loading. Our son, Doug, and daughter, Barbra, who were 11 and five at the time, wanted to be near the action, although I tried to persuade them to stay in the downstairs rumpus room, away from the draft. Everyone was getting very tired and cold when our wonderful neighbors dropped in with a huge pot of coffee and sandwiches. Ken went to move our car from in front of the van, but the car was frozen and wouldn't budge. Once again, the neighbors came to our rescue and in no time had the cables on and the car running again. I'll never forget the warmth of the long-awaited motel room when we arrived—I never wanted to leave it. However, the next day, after a sad farewell to relatives and friends, we made our way north.

In Edson, it was also bitterly cold! We stayed in a hotel that was a rest stop for large diesel truck drivers. It seemed that half the night truckers in their noisy big boots clumped up and down the stairs while their trucks idled noisily all night. Besides having the children in the room, we had our blond cocker spaniel named Casey. He disliked men, so every time he heard footsteps, he'd let out a low growl, and I'd pull him by his leash, which was at the side of my bed, so I could stroke his head and assure him that everything was all right.

It was a wonder that Ken didn't have an angina attack through all this turmoil (the stress of moving, plus facing a bitter cold wind), which often triggers pain in angina sufferers. However, at this time, he had no evidence of heart disease.

We had often reminisced how his sister and brother had died suddenly from heart attacks, and his father had passed away at 60 when Ken was only 16. I, too, had suffered the loss of my father, who, at 60, passed away while visiting my brother John (an R.C.M.P. officer) and his wife Louise in Nova Scotia. I was 17 years old at the time.

Ken's mother had been told by her physician to warn her children to review their lifestyles, as their family tree revealed a long list of cardiac casualties. However, young people think nothing bad will ever happen to them, just to the other person. They live like most, ignoring most of the risk factors that could improve and prolong their lives.

One summer day during this year, we decided to drive

to Hinton to check out shops. We were in the Bay when Ken, after climbing the stairs from the basement to the main floor, suddenly clutched his chest and had to sit down. I noticed that lines seemed etched on his face, which had a grey pallor, perspiration beaded down his forehead. It was scary, as I had seen the same look on my father's face just before he slipped a nitroglycerin pill under his tongue. I asked the children to remain quiet and let their father rest for a second. Soon the pink started coming back into his face, and he said that the pain was subsiding.

Ken insisted it was from indigestion because we had just finished a meal at a local restaurant before going to the Bay, where he had to climb stairs. I was quite certain it was more than that and suggested he see a doctor for a full checkup. However, he shrugged off this advice.

In July, Ken was offered a promotion and a chance to return to Calgary. I'll have to admit I was delighted, as I missed our relatives and friends. Ken had been raised in a small town in Ontario, and I in a small town in Saskatchewan, and now our children, although for a period of just six months, had been able to experience life in a small town. They would like to have stayed longer but were happy when they heard that their dad had found a house across the street from both an elementary and a junior high school, plus a city playground in the same area where we had lived previously.

This move was our tenth in 14 years, seven due to transfers and three to more desirable locations within the city. Two of the transfers were to Charlottetown, P.E.I., one for 11 months in 1970 (our daughter was born there in May) and the other back to the Island in 1972 for nine months, where Hudson's Bay Oil and Gas had a drilling program, initially offshore and the second time onshore. Later, in 1979, my husband was chosen to relieve a co-worker who was transferred to Jakarta, Indonesia. This time we went to Perth, Australia, a beautiful sub-tropical city on the shores of the Indian Ocean in Western Australia.

I know it must have been difficult for Ken to go to Australia, as he is a white-knuckled traveller when it comes to flying, but his desire to go overcame his fear of flying. Flying in small planes did not bother him, but he had an aversion to large commercial aircraft. He left in April, and the children and I flew over in June, when school was out. At age 48, I had only flown previously for a total of one and one-half hours. We had always travelled by car or train when possible. When we flew to Perth, although all arrangements were to be cleared by our company, we were stranded in San Francisco for two days. This experience would fill another book, but we did finally make it to Perth and had a wonderful time there.

Ken found his transfers interesting and challenging, and he was enthusiastic about them all. However, a certain amount of stress is associated with moving children around to new homes, having to make new friends, with the children having to adapt to new school systems.

It was after we returned from Edson that Ken experienced another pain in his chest. This time he was diagnosed as having angina pectoris. When he arrived home after seeing the doctor, he was very depressed as he was sure he was going to die soon. I wasn't surprised at the diagnosis, knowing his family history, but my brain was reeling trying to think of some comforting words. The only thing that I could come up with was, "If you are destined to have heart disease, at least consider it a blessing to get a warning sign. Not everyone gets this message, so that they can change their lifestyle, or if some do, they ignore the signs and then don't make it, or their heart is severely damaged. You should consider yourself lucky to be given the opportunity to change the things in your lifestyle that put pressure on your heart." It's not easy to erase bad habits, but each person has only themselves to blame if they refuse to do it.

1989 is one year I'd like to forget. Ken's angina pains were beginning to be more frequent even after walking short distances. Many times I had to drive him downtown to work and then pick him up later. Finally, something had to be done because the pains and headaches were becoming unbearable.

It's not easy being the spouse of a person suffering from angina. Angina sufferers seem to be very moody, impatient, cranky and can switch from being happy and carefree one moment to being almost mean and miserable the next, no doubt because of the helplessness they experience which leaves them in doubt, weak and in pain.

It was also scary at night, to hear his labored breathing, not knowing whether I should call 911 or not.

The day I met Dr. Aldrete was a tremendous boost to my morale and to my own dwindling patience. He just seemed perfect for the job ahead. I had complete confidence in his ability, which I expressed often to Ken. I just did not picture anything going wrong.

During the period that Ken underwent waiting for his surgery, day-to-day activities were routine, with both Ken and I doing our best to not show any great reason for concern to the children. This was for the most part successful until Christmas Day, 1989. Christmas morning is always an exciting fun time at our house. Ken, like a kid, is always the first one up. It's also his birthday. I usually phone my brother Doug, who lives in an apartment nearby, to hurry over and join us. On this Christmas, however, Ken was the last one up, as if he were hoping we'd skip the day. He just didn't feel like being joyful or enthusiastic. Amidst his gifts he'd received a special sander he'd wanted for his carpentry set. He also received a hockey book that Peter Maher and Theoren Fleury had inscribed when they autographed books in a drugstore one day. I know he appreciated the gifts, but he gave them and us a blank stare, as if to he were thinking, "Why buy all these things—I'll never get to use them." Somehow, we got through the day, but I doubt if he remembers anything about that day or the week following, except for the frequent pains in his chest.

The doctor and nursing staff usually let the patient to be operated on, and his or her spouse or relatives, see another patient in the ICU, so everyone will know what to expect at first glance after the operation. They feel it eases the trauma of witnessing about 10 tubes sprouting out from all parts of a loved one's body. They didn't have anyone booked for an operation on New Year's day, and as Ken was scheduled for 8:00 AM on January 2nd, other arrangements were made.

In this case, I and a woman patient, along with her daughter and son-in-law, were taken to a room where the procedures for the operation were explained. As there was no human patient to show us, they brought out a doll with tubes coming out of it in the same position as they would appear on the patient. Some people wince at this idea, but I found it very helpful. It was rather ironic, and I had to smile as the doll was a Ken doll from the Barbie doll series, and my daughter had these dolls at home. As well, both dolls were the namesakes of my husband and daughter.

The patient cannot have any medication or relaxants the night before, so I knew that Ken was in for a terrible night as anxiety increases heart pain. With great reluctance, the children and I left him alone.

He didn't want me to come before the operation because he knew he would be sedated first thing in the morning. He says now that if he'd known how little he remembered (he didn't even recall going into the operating room), he wouldn't have fussed so much the day before.

Our son and daughter were both starting new jobs, and as I felt nothing was going to go wrong, and nothing they could do would help, I suggested that they go to work and I'd keep them posted. Most of my morning was taken up with answering the phone, as caring relatives and friends from near and far phoned with questions.

It was a relief when Dr. Aldrete phoned around 12:30 to say that Ken had come through the operation and was just fine. I returned as many calls as I could, starting with Doug and Barb, and then headed for the hospital.

When I arrived, Ken had awakened for just a couple of minutes and then drifted off again. Prior to my visit, the spouse of a former patient had told me to expect the worst. She said her husband was lying on his back nude except for a sheet across his privates, and he was pale and cold with tubes everywhere, making him look like he was dead. She was so frightened. But maybe she went in too soon, as Ken's skin seemed pink, and although he was nearly nude, I found it understandable because all the tubes have to be visible to the nurses. I found myself counting the tubes and examining them to see if they were in the same spot as in the doll. I remember saying to the nurse, "I think he's fine, he's snoring."

The nurse had just given him more sedation, so I decided to come back around 5:00. The next time I arrived, he was awake and gave me a smile as best he could with a hose down his throat. I was very proud of him. Here was a man who had been so fidgety, almost obstinate, lying perfectly still like he was supposed to.

Ken's hands were tied loosely down with a bandage to stifle any urge to pull out a tube. He gave a gentle tug with his hand—I looked at the nurse because I thought I wouldn't be allowed to touch him in case I passed on germs from something I may have touched, but she said not to worry. She loosened the bandage and placed a clipboard with a sheet of paper attached to it into his hand and gave him a pencil. He printed "Are you okay?" and "How are the kids?"

I took the clipboard and almost started to write the answers to his questions when I thought, I don't need the clip board; I can talk to him. He doesn't have any tubes in his ears. I guess all the tubes I was trying not to step on or bump confused me for a minute.

He listened intently as I repeated the phone messages from his family in Ontario, as well as from other relatives and friends. I told everyone his skin was a good pink color and he had been snoring, so I was sure he was all right, although his room mates might not be getting much rest. When he tried to smile, the line on the monitor attached to the hose in his throat lurched upward. I suggested he not move his mouth, as it was affecting the monitor, and by moving the hose, he may also injure his throat.

Before going into see him in ICU, I'd made up my mind that I wouldn't have a worried expression on my face, even if there was something to worry about. It wouldn't be good to make him feel anxious when he already felt helpless, being kept immobile. Because he was sedated, he was very calm that first day.

I told the nurse that he usually complains that his feet are cold as he was uncovered. I was surprised he hadn't written "My feet are cold" on the clipboard. I remarked to the nurse that I bet the first thing the next day he wanted was socks on his feet. When I phoned just after 7:00 AM the next morning for his condition, the nurse added, "He wants you to bring him some heavy wool socks." Now I knew his body was trying to return to normal.

The nurse said that she would withdraw the sedative drugs slowly, but that Ken would have to start breathing on his own as soon as possible, so she could remove the hose from down his throat. I wasn't there when the nurses removed his tubes in ICU, but they told me that he never complained about anything hurting, but he was glad to get rid of the tubes. He must have been so relieved he had made it through the operation.

On Thursday at noon, they moved him out of ICU into a ward with one other patient who was going for surgery the next day. This patient was very nervous and the nurses said having Ken in with him was the best thing that could have happened to alleviate his fears.

I was surprised when the nurse suggested she take Ken for a short walk (after such an extensive operation, you don't expect the patient to do this). The more determined patients are to get better, the sooner they are on their feet. Attitude is such an important factor; it promotes healing after any operation, I'm sure.

I visited each day and could see his recovery progressing well. He hugged his small pillow (Teddy they call them) to his chest when exerting energy, as he did when walking, sitting up, coughing, or rolling out of bed by using his elbow to support his weight, a must to get off the bed.

Most of us are vain when it comes to our bodies, and we don't like to hear critical remarks, even if they are true, My husband now had a large scar down his chest and one leg where incisions had been made. Ken never complained to me about these scars, either in the hospital or when he got home. It doesn't bother me either. In fact, they make me thankful that modern medicine has found a way to give renewed life to people who otherwise would be subjected to stifling pain and depression until that final strike.

It was a great feeling to finally watch Ken walk for blocks without experiencing pain. Unless he keeps an eye on his diet and keeps on walking, he could be back to square one, with only himself to blame. One good thing is that he gave up smoking, a bad habit that had haunted him for years. Being on disability, away from some of the stress, made it easier to erase this life-threatening habit.

One sad thing that happened during this stressful period was his beloved cat Boots had to be put to sleep in February, less than one month after Ken came home from the hospital. This old stray had nestled on the bed close to him while he rested before going to the hospital. While Ken was in the hospital, I'd say each night to the cat, "Now Bootie, I know you are ailing, but please try and hang in there till dad is home and well on the road to recovery. You are such a part of his life and ours." Then I'd cuddle him close to me and tell him what a wonderful pet and friend he was to all of us and he'd purr away.

Finally the day came when Boots appeared to be really suffering. We rushed him to the vet, but knew he could do nothing for him. Poor Boots purred, hoping we would take him home.

Wanting to give some comfort to my husband and children during this terrible ordeal, as most pet owners will understand, I suggested that I go in the back room with the veterinarian and his assistant and hold Boots while they gave him an injection, so we wouldn't feel like we had abandoned him. I did this while the family walked back to the car. It felt the right thing for me to do, just as I had felt that my husband's operation was the right course to take.

Hopefully, our children will take heed of the possibilities of heart disease, making themselves aware of the risks and symptoms of the disease. The time to do something about heart disease is now. Forever leaving the preventative measures until tomorrow may be a fatal mistake.

BARBRA

When my dad asked if I would contribute something to his book, I found it difficult to agree to his request. Firstly, I haven't written any type of composition since my school days, and secondly, it was a painful period in my life, and I knew it would be hard to write about it. My dad and I, at that time, had difficulties communicating. Like most teenagers, I wasn't very willing to understand, and I felt emotionally cut off from my mom and dad. The details of the surgery were withheld from my brother and me. I suppose they wanted to spare us any emotional trauma, but not knowing what was really going on probably lessened the significance of the bypass surgery. I've always known my dad to be big, strong and courageous. He put on a front for me, trying to make me believe he was doing okay and wasn't worried about the upcoming event. I didn't even realize, until I began reading this book, how afraid he was and how vulnerable he was feeling. I know I may have given him the impression that I didn't care, but I also didn't understand the seriousness of the operation. I would say the purpose of these contributions from me and my family is to help other people going through the same ordeal. Hopefully they will better understand the procedure and not be uninformed like I was.

I cannot think back to a time when I did not know my father had a heart problem. I can remember my mom ordering us kids to keep quiet and try not to annoy him after he got home from work. His everyday living involved a limited amount of physical activity, and he could not handle the smallest amount of exertion without experiencing fatigue. I remember him taking a drug called nitroglycerin. Other than saying at times that he had a pain in his chest, Dad never openly displayed any signs of illness. All I knew, at a young age, was that he was frequently irritable, angry and depressed. I can see now that his condition contributed so much to his dark moods. One cannot be happy and cheerful when full of pain. I knew, even then, that he desperately needed to change his lifestyle. Smoking, lack of exercise, ignoring any warnings about high calories and carbohydrates, and perhaps one of the most dominating factors in heart disease—extreme worry and stress—were all contributing factors. I was so proud of my father when he eventually quit smoking and began watching his diet. It was perhaps at this point that he believed he really wanted to live.

The two months previous to Dad's surgery had been

emotionally hard on our family. We were all worried. I remember him being so strong and trying so hard to be positive. There was never a doubt in my mind that he wouldn't make it through the operation. I never allowed myself to believe that he could actually die or that anything could go wrong. I held onto the hope that he would be just fine. The surgery was scheduled for January 2, 1990, and I sensed my father's apprehension about the bypass. Perhaps if he had the opportunity to read a book such as this one, he would have understood more of what he had to go through, both physically and mentally. Maybe he could have been more emotionally aware and realized that it was okay to be scared. It must have taken a great deal of energy to cover up his feelings for the benefit of me and my brother. The only time my dad openly became distraught was on Christmas day of 1989. The season and the wonderful peacefulness only Christmas can give us was in the air around us. My family and I were joined around the tree opening our gifts. I noticed a couple of times that Dad was not really interested in opening his presents—he was watching all of us with ours. It was like he was forming a memory of his family to cherish. I know now he believed this was the last Christmas he would be with us. It all became too much for Dad to observe this scene and think these thoughts, and he silently began to cry. I remember sensing my dad's despair and wishing I could help him somehow. That night, for the first time in a long time, I prayed to God to spare him, and then I cried myself to sleep.

I remember at this time feeling a great deal of guilt for a few reasons. One was that I had difficulties telling my dad how much I loved him. I felt I could have supported him more. As well, I had planned and booked a tropical vacation months before. We were due to leave for Jamaica on January 12th—just 10 days after Dad's operation. When I asked him if I should change my plans, he repeatedly encouraged me not to. I speculated that both my parents believed it would be good for me to get away from the tension and sickness that had engulfed us all. I kept my plans with the intention to cancel if it turned out that I was needed at home.

My dad was admitted to the Holy Cross Hospital two days before his operation. I did not see him for four days. Immediately after the surgery, when my dad was in ICU, only my mom was there for him. They decided my brother and me shouldn't have to see all the machines and tubes, which they felt would probably terrify us. The first night I saw him, he was sitting up in a chair. I think at this point, he still didn't believe he'd made it through. Here before me sat a changed man. I sensed it then, and the change has become increasingly apparent even up to this day. My dad, Doug and I walked down the hallway—Dad walked very, very slowly and had to rest several times. His leg and chest had stitches that looked like staples. I was surprised at how he looked. I was expecting the worst, but he really appeared to be in control, and I suppose was greatly relieved. Each time I visited my dad in the hospital, I could see the improvements he was making. I knew he had a long way to go, yet his new positive attitude made him somewhat invincible and able to get through anything. I left on schedule for Jamaica, feeling confident and self-assured that he was going to be all right.

Nearly three years have passed since then, and I now look back and realize the importance of the family unit, which I had taken for granted. We depend on each other for love, security and support. I feel much closer to my dad now than I did before his operation. We understand each other better. I was so proud of my dad during his recuperation period. He changed his lifestyle and his way of thinking. He's much more positive and ambitious. He's spunky, optimistic, open-minded and cheerful. He has set many new goals and has dedicated a lot of his time to helping people go through the same traumatic event. He's learned how to handle stress better, and he's become more patient. I have no doubt that this experience has made him a stronger, better person, and I would like to give thanks to the doctors and to God for giving my father a second chance on life.

DOUG

Okay, Dad, here it is! Finally, my thoughts going onto paper—it's not too easy to get me to do anything, is it? But after 27 years, I would have to think that you're getting used to it. When you think back, we kids used to challenge your patience all the time, and probably still do the odd time. It's a game kids play—seeing how mad they can make their parents, making sure at all times that they have easy access to the outside door. If the cycle repeats itself, I'm sure my turn will come some day. I sometimes think, with some sorrow, about how much stress we probably caused you and if it related to your eventual surgery.

I wondered how serious you were when you talked about writing a book. I mean, you did mention building a hot tub a few times—I still don't see one. Then there was the famous line "This weekend I'm going to organize that damn basement!" Were we surprised to find it as cluttered as ever after you cleaned it? Other projects have come and gone, but I must give you credit, you sure stuck to your guns on this one.

Going back to the times before your surgery is difficult, but here is my attempt.

I do recall Barb and me picking you up at the hospital after you had your angiogram. You were tested for the percentage of blockage in your arteries, and when you found out it was very serious, you never let on to us! Dads just don't get scared, right? Two months later, when you booked your triple bypass operation, I believe my immediate reaction was something like "Oh, well, things could be worse."

Now this casual attitude about the whole issue was just me. I try to be positive about things because I feel that in today's world you pretty well have to. You may have wondered by my reaction if I really cared at all. In fact, Dad, I was just plain ignorant. Of course, I cared, but for some reason I did not think that triple bypass surgery was that serious. I mean, with all the operations performed over the years, the doctors knew exactly what they were doing, right? I now realize that such an operation is very serious.

Your operation date was set for January 2, 1990. My first realization of what you were going through came to me on Christmas Day. It was a typical Christmas for us— you, Mom, Uncle Doug, Barb, me and, of course, the pets. We all gathered around the tree to open the abundance of presents we usually had. It was then that I noticed you seemed quite content just sitting in your chair, watching everyone shredding Christmas paper. Just then a strange thing happened—you broke down and started to cry. Mom immediately ran over to console you, and I was in shock! Dads don't cry, do they? Barb and I had never witnessed this before. It hit home hard that you were indeed scared, and as you revealed to us after your operation, you thought that this could be your last Christmas with us. I just wished at that time that there was a way that I could have helped.

Pets are a very important part of the Burton clan. For those of you who have pets, you know what I'm talking about. As mentioned before in this book, our pets have all been strays. My cat is no different. My sister Barb was responsible for his adoption. I was having some friends over one night, and Barb noticed a cat hanging out in the front of my apartment. She observed how affectionate the cat was and brought it up to my apartment. I said, "NO" because we already had a kitten. She snuck him in anyway, and he ended up staying the night. After six years, he's still with me. I named him Casper. He was pure white and friendly, just like Casper the ghost. I think we all thank

God that Barb never got a job in a pet store—she would have brought home a new pet every day.

When Dad was sick, my parents had the three pets, Rocky, Buddy and the loveable Boots, the cat that kept everyone in line. Pets are very significant because they sometimes communicate when we can't. I really believe that they were instrumental in Dad getting through his operation. They were always by his side when we couldn't be. And I know if I were ever worried about something, I would confide in Rocky or Boots, and I knew they were always ready to listen. They didn't give much advice, but it was a great way to get things off my chest. Dad must have felt the same way. While I'm glad that our pets played such an important role, I'm even happier that since Dad's operation, our family has learned more about how to talk to each other. I think there are two types of families: those who confide in each other and those who don't. Before Dad's surgery, we fell somewhere in the middle—we were concerned with each other and always kept in touch, but we didn't always discuss things that may have been bothering us. Maybe this was why it was tough for Dad to tell us how frightened he was.

The day of the operation finally came, and I waited and waited for Mom to call with the news. While the operation was taking place, I wasn't as scared as I thought I would be—I just had this feeling that Dad would come through it with flying colors. And what do you know—I was right!

Mom reported one incident that assured me Dad was on the road to recovery. Now there are a lot of hockey-crazed fans out there, but I never heard anything like this. Mom says that when Dad awoke, after writing on a paper attached to a clipboard enquiring about us and asking if she was okay, he wrote "Did the Flames win?" The astonished nurse replied, "I believe they tied." Dad's next question, "Who scored the goals?" sent the nurse scurrying around for the day's sports section of the newspaper, so

STRAIGHT FROM THE HEART   113

she could answer that question. I couldn't believe it! He didn't ask, "Am I alive?" or "Are you an Angel?" He just wanted to know how Calgary's hockey team was doing.

On my first visit to Dad after his operation, he was obviously very weak, and this was hard to take, because he was usually quite active, except for his periods of pain during an angina attack. However, the second time I visited, I could see that he was again completely in control of himself. He knew practically everyone on the hospital floor, which didn't surprise me, because he'd usually talk to any stranger as though he or she was his best friend. The three people I remember most were his hospital roommates. When I walked into his room one night, they were all sitting up in their beds talking like buddies gathered around a card table on poker night. I think it was essential for him to have these roommates to talk to. They had that common bond that grows out of going through the same thing together. They all knew what scared them and what comforted them, and they came together as a team, psyching themselves up for that big new game of life after surgery.

Dad always maintained absolute confidence and, most importantly, a positive attitude. I was pleased with this display of confidence. The nurses proclaimed that he was an inspiration to everyone, and you wouldn't believe how proud I was of him at that moment. I knew right then and there that he would make an excellent ambassador for anyone else who required bypass surgery, or any surgery for that matter. His involvement with Heart to Heart is very beneficial to a lot of people I'm sure, but writing this book was probably the best idea he ever had.

After I read these stories, I became aware that I was not the only person in our family that was exposed to emotional stress while undergoing this illness. It made me wish that I had been more aware of this and had done something to alleviate some of this trauma.

There are, however, positive results to offset negative ones. In my case, having bypass surgery brought us closer together as a family and, as Barb stated, we now understand one another better. Doug wondered if stress was caused by the actions they exhibited during their growing up. My reply to this is that there is no way I would trade the experience in life of being able to watch these two develop from birth—helpless and dependent on others—to the mature adults they now are. I am proud to be their father.

I know that the feeling I now have is so much more positive than before, a feeling that has been strengthened by the support of my family.

God's Three Strays

One evening I was thinking about Boots, our cat, whom we had to have euthanized (put to death in a painless way for reasons of mercy) one month after my surgery. Because he was quite old and had cancer of the liver, the vet said we would be extending no kindness by subjecting him to an operation at his age. It was a decision I did not want to make, and hopefully I will never have to again.

My thoughts turned to words, and I started writing a short verse about our beloved cat. As this lyric appeared on paper, a feeling of continuing on included our two dogs and produced the poem "God's Three Strays." Friends who have read this poem have expressed such interest and encouragement that I have included it in this book.

I wrote "God's Three Strays" to show how the emotions of one family can be affected by pets. These sentiments are also displayed again and again by others, and affect the psychological well-being of those who are ill, old, confined and/or lonely.

It is quite possible that you have read or heard stories of the love and devotion animals give to people in need. Many people who have been seriously ill, old, lonely or depressed to the point where their desire to continue on in life has expired, then a dog, cat, or some other little creature enters the scene and their depression disappears.

It is becoming more evident that some individuals confined (in prisons or mental hospitals) who have a history of violence will, when exposed to an animal (or a bird, a reptile or a fish) become docile and are much easier to deal with. One example of this was projected in the movie *The Birdman of Alcatraz.*

Children who have lost one or both parents sometimes go into a psychological shell and show no interest in day-to-day activities. Then they become attached to some creature, finally having found something that will love them and give them that sense of security they either lost or never did have. Here again, the temperament of the individual changes—sometimes drastically.

There are always stories and statistics appearing in print about heart disease and the affect pets have on people with this problem. Just this morning, a story appeared in the *Calgary Sun* about a hospital in Melbourne, Australia, that has found that pet owners are less likely to suffer from heart disease than people who don't own animals. It further states that people with a pet had lower blood pressure and lower cholesterol levels than those who did not. The research goes on to say that the health of pet owners differed than that of other people, but couldn't explain how pets exactly affected health.

Our three pets were, as the poem states, three strays who came from nowhere. Boots showed up in our backyard one summer day in 1979. Both my children, Doug and Barb, had always wanted a pet, but we moved around frequently because I was employed in the oil industry. Renting was usually an easier and more desirable method to obtain accommodation and having no pets was frequently a stipulation in acquiring a residence. As we now owned our own home, and Bootie did not express any desire to move on, he became a permanent fixture, despite efforts to locate his owner. I am certain that Doug had a hand in helping Boots make up his mind about where he wanted to homestead, but he didn't let Dad in on this important decision. Marion said she would look out to the backyard, and on two successive days Dougie was lying on the lawn beside the cat, petting him. Barbie was also a partner in this conspiracy.

After Boots moved in, he took command of the household, and as is the manner with the feline species, he would do what he wanted to do and that was that. It never ceases to amaze me how independent cats can be. Yet dogs are the exact opposite and will do practically anything requested to please their masters. Even so, with this vast difference in attitudes, in our household we always gave the same feeling of love to either cat or dog as each had his own way of capturing our affection.

Approximately one year after Boots showed up, Rocky just as mysteriously appeared on the scene. He landed on our front doorstep—Barb was captivated, and the two of them shared an immediate mutual affection. Rocky then took off as though he had one important item on his agenda to complete before making the commitment of settling into his new home. We thought we would never see him again, but he reappeared the next day at our door, and then I am certain my daughter had a heart-to heart-discussion with Rocky to convince him that he should settle down and grow roots with our family.

Despite all our efforts to locate Rocky's owner, we were never successful. On two occasions, people came in response to our ad in the paper, but they discovered that it was not their dog. Both times they phoned before coming over, and in the interim before they arrived, tears of anguish were flowing from my daughter who felt she was certain to lose her new-found friend. Her mother tried to convince her that we could not keep a pet that belonged to someone else, but this rationalization could not penetrate the mind of a ten-year-old girl who loved animals. Rocky's owners never were located, to the joy of Barb, and the two of them became inseparable.

It was inevitable that Rocky join PALS. PALS (Pet Access League Society) is a Calgary organization that has professional handlers and veterinarians screen pets for information about health, training and personality. Barb knew that Rocky had so much love to give that she wanted him to share it with others. So Rocky has, for some years, visited a Calgary nursing home and given this love to the elderly. Buddy (our other pet) may join him in this venture, although at present, there is a waiting list to join PALS.

PALS is now in its 10th year of operation. The following is information taken from their brochure:

Expanding steadily since its inception in the spring of 1982, the PVP (pet visitation program) now provides regular pet visits to over 4,000 residents and patients in 29 Calgary hospitals, nursing homes, a correctional centre and other care facilities.

Pet owners recognize, and medical evidence confirms, the therapeutic value of interaction between humans and animals.

Pets provide unqualified love and acceptance with no regard to age, appearance or handicap.

Pets evoke responses from people who may respond to nothing else.

Pets don't judge, criticize, disagree or talk back.

Scientific studies demonstrate blood pressure drops and stress levels are greatly reduced when we stroke or talk to pets.

Dr. Leo K. Bustad, Washington State University (Founder of Animal Assisted Therapy) states: "Close relationships link all living things in the environment, but the forces that connect people and animals are especially strong and enduring."

The stories that could be told of incidents occurring between these pets and the people they help are so numerous that they could create an entire book.

Buddy was the third member of the animal world to come into our family at this period in our lives. One cold March day four years ago (it was about 20 below), Barb was at work when this ugly old mutt appeared outside looking very frightened and cold, lonely and hungry. As was her nature, she immediately took to this vagabond that most people would have shooed away or ignored. She gave him half her lunch, and later in the day Buddy was still outside, looking in at the only person in the world who seemed to care for him. Before it was time to leave for the day, Barb checked the phone book and found the only place that she could turn to for help for her new-found friend, Animal Control. She thought it was similar to the S.P.C.A. (Society for the Prevention of Cruelty to Animals), but unfortunately, it turned out to be the dog pound. When the animal control officer arrived, Barb asked him what would happen to Buddy, and he replied that if he were not claimed in four days, he would be put to sleep. Her feeling of elation turned to devastation, and she came home with tears in her eyes. She cried all during the night until her mother said they would both go to the pound if he were not claimed in the allotted time, and bring him home to try to find either his owner or a new home.

A word of caution is inserted here so that others do not go through this same unfortunate experience. If you find an animal in distress and want to help, contact the Humane Society (S.P.C.A.). They are always available to give that tender care to these unfortunates.

Marion and Barb went to the pound on the designated day—Barb with a wish that the mutt was not picked up by anyone, so that she would have another pet, despite that her mother told her her dad would never allow this to happen. This didn't deter Barb one iota because she knew that was the smallest problem she now encountered. Knowing how she could twist her father around her little finger, she resolved to bring the old man around to her way of thinking later. As they walked past the cages, dogs barked and wagged their tails, hoping they would be the chosen one to be released from their prison. They finally came to Buddy's cage. He lay, half dead and showing no emotion whatsoever. He had diarrhea and was practically starving. Even though his dish was full, it appeared he lost all desire for food, but he did manage to look up at the two with those beautiful brown eyes that had captivated Barb's heart in the first place.

Paying the $105 fee (for shots, license and fine), Barb became the custodian of a pet that wasn't expected to live. They brought him home and, and because it was still freezing cold, we turned the furnace on in the garage, and put a mat and blanket on the floor for him to lie on. He made no movement from Saturday to Tuesday. Marion got little bits of food down him on the end of a straw—she made a mixture of kaopectate and cottage cheese. She said later she was afraid that if she opened his mouth and tried to feed him with a spoon, he might be vicious and try to bite her. With the little strength he had in his poor little body, I don't think he could have bitten anyone or anything.

Marion warned Barbra to expect the worst when they went out to see this poor animal each morning because Marion was certain that he would not be alive. However, one morning as they entered the garage, Buddy opened those same brown eyes that had charmed Barb originally, and gave his tail a feeble wag. He eventually ate some chicken and then some ground hamburger, and gradually he regained his desire for food.

Rocky was finally allowed to see Buddy, and he greeted his new friend with an exuberance that overwhelmed Buddy, who was so weak that his attempt to respond to Rocky's friendliness caused him to collapse on the floor.

Each day Buddy grew stronger, and as we never did find the owner, and I don't remember any attempt made to try to adopt him out to anyone, he became the third member of our menagerie. The ugly old mutt grew more beautiful with each passing day and as much loved as our other two domestics.

We thought Buddy was a "Heinz 57" type of animal because he didn't resemble any breed of dog that we could identify. A friend of ours, George Cairns, was visiting with his daughter Tracey one day. She was so intrigued by his appearance that she did some research and discovered that in reality he was a thoroughbred—a Basset Griffon Vendeen. This animal is raised in Europe and used for hunting wild boars and deer. Trained as a hunter, he is mean and vicious; domesticated, he is tender and loving— an ideal dog for children. True to his breeding, the domesticated Buddy never growls or snaps at anyone, and instantly laps up attention from wherever he can get it. Rocky, with the same disposition, became his instant companion, and they spend many happy hours romping around and wrestling with each other. With his new found royalty status, we decided to change our title from the "ugly old mutt" to "Sir Bud." However, those who are on a friendly basis with him are still permitted to call him Buddy.

It was always interesting to discover what names Doug and Barb would come up for their pets. Boots was named for his pronounced white paws—he was a black cat with white markings on his chest and paws; Rocky was designated as such because of the movie out by that name at the time; and Buddy because he was just that—a buddy to Rocky.

When I became sick with angina, and during the two month waiting period for my operation as well as the month after, Boots seemed to sense my need for condolence and very seldom left my side. As previously stated, poor Bootie was sick himself. a problem that we were not aware of at the time. One month after my operation, the most painful decision of my life was made as he was put to rest to end his suffering from cancer.

Rocky was always Barbie's dog, and Buddy seemed to sense the vacuum created by Boot's departure, so he took over where our cat left off. He never leaves my side, and when I sit, he will stay beside me with his foot on mine, so that if I move, he won't be left behind. He follows me everywhere, and when I think of how close this loveable animal came to either dying or being put to death at the pound because no-one except Barb cared, I give thanks that he was directed to our home, and for the joy he has brought into our hearts. As the poem states, it's apparent that God was looking over Buddy and destined this loveable dog for our family.

GOD'S THREE STRAYS

They came to us
We know not why
It seemed God sent them
From the sky

First there was Boots
The obstinate cat
He had his own ways
And that was that

And then came Rocky
No love would be spared
He had that manner
To show how he cared

Third was Buddy
The ugly old mutt
However in time
He was anything but

A home they did find
To care for their needs

God has his own way
To do these kind deeds

As the kids grew older
You could see what it meant
To have these three pets
That God had sent

Dougie grew up
And left our nest
He left his pets
He knew this was best

And then I was sick
But it was a joy to see
The three pets around
To comfort me

After my bypass
When I came home
Bootie stayed close
He didn't roam

Our cat was sick
It never entered our minds
He waited for me
Before showing the signs

Again it was God
Who kept him here
Until I was better
And over my fear

Now Bootie has gone
He was put to sleep
We miss him so
Our sorrow is deep

Barbie then left
But she couldn't roam
Without taking Rocky

To share her new home

We're left with Buddy
Just Mom and I
It's nice he's around
The loveable guy

Our pets were work
We knew it would be
But life is much better
To have had these three

When I have to go
And make my amends
God please let me be
With my three friends

PETER AND DEM

Different Patients, Different Feelings

This story illustrates the emotional trauma a cardiac patient undergoes, both before and after surgery. In this instance, one patient, Peter, had undergone bypass surgery, while the other, Dem, had yet to cope with the experience.

It is a requirement to obtain clearances from people when you use their names in print. As I was unable to locate one of the patients used in this chapter to obtain this necessary documentation, I have identified him as Peter Lakusta, which is a pseudonym.

Post-heart surgery depression is predominant in cardiac patients, and June Pimm, a psychologist at the University of Miami who had studied heart patients afflicted with lingering depression, says that cardiac patients are more likely to experience emotional problems than people undergoing other major operations. The reason, she believes, is due to the heart's deep emotional significance. Pimm, who wrote the *Heart Survey Handbook* after an 1984 study showed that short-term counselling helps eliminate depression following coronary bypass surgery says, "You lose confidence and become anxious and depressed."

"Anything can happen at that point," she states. "You can lose interest in your activities. You can lose interest in your sex life. You can decide that you want to get a divorce, that you hate the woman you've been married to for 30 years. Everybody has their own way of responding. Much of the time these seemingly extreme responses are signs of depression.

Pimm wrote her book after a 1984 study showed that short term counselling helps eliminate depression following coronary bypass surgery.

American studies suggest that depression occurs surprisingly often, affecting up to 30 percent of coronary bypass patients as long as three years after surgery. Pimm says she suspects the statistics are similar in Canada, where about 12,000 patients have open-heart surgery each year.

On the third Wednesday evening of each month, the Heart to Heart Support Society meets at the General Hospital in Calgary. This society consists of a group of people whose lives have been changed by the effects of heart disease, who have volunteered to share the benefit of their experiences with those who are presently undergoing these problems. They visit patients in hospital and after discharge if required, as well as assisting families and friends of these people. In addition, an objective of the Society is to educate the public to the risks of heart disease. They also raise monies for cardiac research and education.

Although, I visited patients only at the Holy Cross Hospital, Fran Hintze, coordinator for these visits at both the Holy Cross and Rockyview Hospitals at the time, asked me if I would go to the Rockyview to see two patients about to undergo bypasses. Although one of our members had already visited the two, this member had a heart attack but had not undergone bypass surgery, so he could not relate to them on the same level as a person who had this operation. Fran advised me of the names of the two patients: Mr. Lakusta and Mr. Dem.

At the hospital, I was to contact Peggy Tan, nurse in charge of the ward where these two were patients. When I approached the reception desk, I was advised that Peggy was on her coffee break. I identified myself to the nurse on duty (although I did have a Calgary District Hospital I.D. on, a prerequisite for visiting patients for this purpose) and gave her the reason for my visit. Her response to my introduction was, "Oh, Mr. Lakusta has had complications and is extremely ill, and I do not think he will be allowed visitors. I will have to check with his nurse before we can make any decision on whether or not you can visit him." Fine, I thought, no problem. At this time, however, Peggy returned from her break, and I introduced myself to her. "Just go ahead in and see Mr. Lakusta," she said, at which time her assistant reminded her that Mr. Lakusta was extremely ill. Peggy replied that we were regarded in the same category as clergy and advised me to proceed with my visit.

I entered Mr. Lakusta's room, where he was curled up in bed in a fetal position looking like he had lost his best friend. The instant I was in the room, he popped out of bed. I almost wanted to run and get a nurse, ring the nursing station, or do something to bring professional help to this man who was so desperately ill—I didn't want him dropping dead on my account!

Instead, however, I introduced myself, and when I told Mr. Lakusta that I had triple bypass surgery, he treated me like a long-lost brother and asked me to call him Peter. He was 75 and had undergone a triple bypass in Montreal 10 years previously, and this factor instantly created the bond so common among cardiac alumnae. Peter was a Ukrainian who had been in the Russian army during World War II. As I had been in the air force, we had another common experience to enhance our relationship. He talked about the extreme cold in 1942 when men froze to death if they dared fall asleep, and when food in the Russian army was at times non-existent. He was an extremely interesting gentleman, and, as is the case when meeting a lot of people with heart problems, I felt rewarded from meeting him and hearing of his experiences.

I saw him twice more, and then he was discharged. He never did have another bypass, and at present is recuperating at this home. The best medicine for him, I thought, was to have someone to talk to. He was in a private room, very lonely, and it appeared that he needed that psychological assistance so many of us can use to alleviate the feeling of depression when confronted with cardiac problems.

Unfortunately, Peter's wife had passed away about four years ago. She was to undergo a bypass operation but was too terrified to go through with the procedure and refused it. Peter said he was home one afternoon resting (at the time he owned a restaurant where he resided) when his daughter came in and gave him the sorrowful news of his wife's sudden demise at the restaurant where she had been helping out. Not having the operation proved fatal to her.

After visiting Peter for over an hour (I had intended to stay from 10 to 15 minutes), it was time to see Mr. Dem. The information Fran received was that this patient was of Chinese descent and spoke very little English. I had also been told that he was emotionally distraught and extremely upset over the forthcoming operation (join the clan).

I walked into the room and lying in bed was the typical waiting-for-an-operation type of patient—he was staring at the ceiling and probably wondering what was in store for him. After the customary introduction about the reason for my visit, I told him that I had undergone a triple bypass and he immediately perked up. He asked me to call him Dem, not Mr. Dem. I later discovered that this was the customary salutation used by orientals. Dem was Vietnamese, not Chinese, and contrary to what Fran had been told, his knowledge of English presented practically no problem whatsoever. He was soft-spoken, amiable, with an infectious smile that created in me an immediate liking for him. He was 53 years old, and had two sons, 16 and 18. His wife had died in Vietnam when the youngest son was only one year old.

Fran's information on Dem's emotional condition was not, however, exaggerated, and when I talked to him, I saw myself two years earlier, waiting for that inevitable approach to doom. He did not think he would survive the operation, and his greatest concern was for the welfare of his two sons, who would be left alone. I spent a good half-hour with him, and when I left, I felt I had penetrated his pessimistic approach to surgery, and that he now realized that he had a chance of survival. He was scheduled for surgery in 10 days, and I asked him if he wanted me to visit him again before his operation. His reply was one of emphatic acceptance.

During the period Dem was in Rockyview (he was moved to the Holy Cross two days before the operation) I continued to visit him. One evening as I was visiting, a woman (the wife of a patient about to undergo angioplasty) approached Dem's bed and asked him the nature of his illness. When he replied, her facial expression was one of horror, and she stated how awful it was to undergo such a procedure and how sorry she felt for him. At this time, I would have liked to have given her a swift kick in the rear. I asked her if she had ever undergone cardiac surgery and when she replied in the negative, I expressed puzzlement at her reply. I told her that I had gone through the experience and outlined a very brief description of the procedure, emphasizing the absence of any feeling during the immediate post-surgery period. In all fairness to this woman, she did not realize the harm she was creating with her remarks, and she was, in fact, a very likeable person. She was astounded that I had undergone such an operation, looked so healthy and had such a positive outlook on life. I am certain that she did not mean to harm Dem with her acrimonious remarks.

After having been exposed to the benefit of encouraging comments from others, and knowing the psychological damage derogatory conversation creates in those on the verge of panic, it would be gratifying to know that anyone coming in contact with someone about to undergo any traumatic experience would be optimistic. I feel quite certain the majority of people would comply with this request if they knew what a difference a cheerful and positive attitude could do to a patient's temperament.

When Dem moved to the Holy Cross hospital, I visited him the day before the operation, at which time he remarked that he did not want his two sons visiting him in ICU (Intensive Care Unit) and seeing the tubes in him. When I asked him if he wanted me to visit him there, he readily agreed. As only immediate family are allowed in ICU, I had to obtain permission from the nursing staff so I contacted Janice Stewart, who made the necessary arrangements for this special request.

Dem had his operation on a Thursday afternoon. When I phoned Friday, I was advised that he was quite groggy, so I waited until Saturday morning to call on him. He was sitting up in a chair when I saw him, and, because he appeared very tired, I spent only a short time with him and left. I had my regular visitation to the cardiac floor the following Tuesday and visited him as well as others. After a six-week recuperation period, he returned to work.

I feel my involvement in these situations is one way to repay those who helped me when I needed it. It would please me if others who have had exposure to open-heart surgery would pass on their experiences, and try to alleviate the tension of those yet to be subjected to this operation.

The Next Step

Once again, I have imposed upon a medical professional, a nurse, Karen Mierau, who has graciously consented to take time from a busy day-to-day schedule to provide an overview of risk factors and to describe the benefits of a cardiac rehabilitation program.

When I went through the cardiac rehab program, Karen was my primary nurse. If I had any questions or fears during this period, she was always there to give assistance.

Karen is a staff nurse in the Cardiac Rehabilitation Program for Southern Alberta at the Calgary General Hospital. She graduated from the Guelph General Hospital, School of Nursing, Guelph, Ontario, and worked in various Intensive Care Units in Saskatchewan and Ontario for the first 10 years of her nursing career. After moving to Alberta in 1981, she became Assistant Head Nurse of the Cardiovascular Ward at the Holy Cross Hospital in Calgary. She then returned to university full-time and received her Bachelor of Nursing degree from the University of Calgary in 1987. Since then, she has been helping cardiac patients focus on their lifestyle at the Cardiac Rehabilitation Program for Southern Alberta.

Here is Karen's account of risk factors and how a cardiac rehab program can assist you in reducing some of these factors in your life:

The Cardiac Rehabilitation Program for Southern Alberta began in 1980 at the Calgary General Hospital. The foresight of a cardiologist who had a special interest in this area of cardiac care, some very generous donations from the Heritage Savings and Trust Fund, and one individual with heart disease, who wished to help others with the same problem made this program a reality. Since then it has been serving 400 to 500 residents of Calgary and Southern Alberta each year who have suffered from angina, heart attacks or have undergone open-heart surgery.

Experiencing any one of these heart-related illnesses can be very traumatic and often causes individuals to reflect on their future as well as their past, considering what they can do and should have done differently. You may have had treatment that improved your situation: medication, angioplasty, coronary artery bypass surgery, or even artherectomy or laser therapy (as our research and technological advances in cardiac care increase our options). A cardiologist having reviewed your situation and the results of various tests performed, will institute the appropriate treatment(s). These interventions are attempting to eliminate your symptoms. However, it is most important to remember that they don't remove the cause of your problem. The blockages in your coronary arteries can come back to haunt you if you do not take a very serious look at what you are doing to yourself on a daily basis.

Heart disease is mainly a disease of choice! Does this come as a shock to you? Granted, you have no control over some risk factors. Family history, for instance, can have a major impact. So can diabetes, age, gender and the fact that you may have already developed a heart problem. The good news is that you can significantly influence a whole range of other risk factors.

That's where cardiac rehabilitation can really enter the picture. The Big Four (the four risk factors with the most dramatic influence) are smoking, hypertension (high blood pressure), sedentary lifestyle (lack of exercise) and elevated cholesterol. If you have a problem in any of these areas, you have some serious work to do. The best thing you can do is to STOP SMOKING if you haven't already done so. The impact of continuing to smoke could be catastrophic! Remember that feeling of impending doom the first you were confronted with a heart problem? I know you don't want it to become a reality. Sounds like scare tactics, right? Maybe so, but it's a fact. You increase your risk of further problems by two to four times if you continue to smoke.

Talk to your doctor and get help. Kick the habit, get your blood pressure under control, follow a heart-healthy diet to get your cholesterol levels within normal range, and start a program of regular exercise. Your doctor will help to ensure that you are on the right track.

Carrying extra pounds around puts an extra strain on your heart and makes daily activities more difficult. If you are 50 pounds overweight, think of putting 50 pounds into a backpack and carrying it around with you wherever you go (you have probably noticed that some people prefer to wear front packs—or should I say porches). This would quickly become tiresome, and you would be tempted to throw your pack into the nearest corner. Every pound you take out of your pack is one less that you have to carry around with you and supply with oxygen and nutrients (your heart's job). So give your heart a break—decrease your intake (only YOU can monitor what and how much you put into your mouth), and increase your output (do moderately challenging aerobic exercise four to six times per week for 30-40 minutes). Consult with your cardiologist about this before you start your exercise program, and sign up for a Cardiac Rehabilitation Program if it's available in your area.

Stress can also significantly influence the condition of your heart. In many cases, it's more the way we cope with stress that causes problems than the stress itself. Some people have a bad day if the doorbell and the phone ring at the same time, while others can cope with immense pressures and come out smiling. It's really a matter of choice and learning new skills that help you cope better.

Professional instruction in stress management techniques can be a major step in reducing stress. Maybe you get more upset than you need to over little things. Ask yourself "Is this life-threatening?" Take time each day to relax and reflect on yourself and those around you. You may find it surprisingly refreshing and enlightening.

The years go by very quickly. Why waste them racing around? After all, you and your loved ones are the most important part of your life. Spend time together, and the rest of your time will be more relaxed and enjoyable as well. Is your 12 hour workday your employer's expectation or your own struggle for perfection? Talk to your doctor about seeing a psychologist or social worker to help sort out your priorities. You could discover a whole new meaning to life.

At the Cardiac Rehabilitation Program for Southern Alberta, we offer a multi-disciplinary approach to lifestyle change. We have experts in each area related to heart disease who can help sort out concerns—dietitians, social workers, a psychologist, an occupational therapist and cardiac nurses. We encourage individuals to choose one or two areas of concern and concentrate on them first. You can't change your whole lifestyle instantly—it's just too overwhelming! As you master one area, such as stopping smoking, you can then change your focus to another concern, such as managing stress more effectively.

Regular exercise is very helpful in increasing your success in several areas. Walking, biking or swimming regularly not only increases your fitness level, but they are a great stress release. They also help you lose weight, giving you more energy as well as an increased sense of well-being. Check with your doctor before starting any kind of regular exercise program and then HAPPY WALKING!

Your future depends upon what you make of it, so good luck and TAKE GOOD CARE OF YOURSELF.

Proper Diet and Nutrition

Marie Toone is a dietitian at Calgary Cardiac Rehab. She helped me with my weight problem over my three month rehabilitation period, and she has graciously consented to pass on some of her expertise in this area.

Marie graduated from the Brigham Young University in Provo, Utah, with a Bachelor of Science degree in Food Science and Nutrition, and went on to complete her Dietetic Internship at the Calgary General Hospital. After spending seven years working in Hawaii, she returned to Calgary to work at the Calgary Rehabilitation Program for Southern Alberta. She comments:

I have been with the Cardiac Rehabilitation Program as a Registered Dietitian for the past 10 years. Looking back, I have seen and talked to over 2,000 people—asking them what they ate, how they prepared their food, where they shop for groceries, where and how often they eat out, if they consume alcohol, coffee or tea, if they use salt, and if they use vitamin or mineral supplements.

All these questions, plus many more, help me to evaluate their eating habits and determine their total fat, saturated fat and cholesterol as well as their alcohol and caffeine intake.

It is well known that elevated blood cholesterol levels are one of the risk factors for the development of heart disease. In addition to looking at total cholesterol, we also look at the level of HDLs (high density lipoproteins), which protect against the development of heart disease. HDLs transport cholesterol away from the tissues to the liver where it can be eliminated from the body. LDLs (low density lipoproteins), on the other hand, transport cholesterol circulating in the blood stream to the cells. This leads to the development of atheroschlerosis.

In 1988, the Canadian Consensus Conference on Cholesterol set out guidelines for cholesterol management:

GOAL LEVELS
(millimoles/Litre)

Total Cholesterol	18 – 29 years	30 years or more
less than 2 risk factors	5.7 or less	6.2 or less
2 or more risk factors	4.6 or less	5.2 or less
HDL	0.9 or more	0.9 or more
LDL	3.0 or less	3.4 or less

My responsibility as a dietitian is to help people modify their eating habits and assist them in maintaining a healthy diet that is low in fat and cholesterol. Dietary changes are a first line defense, especially if a person has elevated cholesterol and/or LDL levels.

When patients comes to see a dietitian, they come for different reasons—some because they are told to do so, others because they want help and information on making changes to their diet.

Some will say, "Where do I start?" or, "Just tell me what to do, and I'll do it." Others say that I have ruined their lives because they feel they are not allowed to eat their favorite meals any longer. Still others say, "Changing my diet won't make me live longer; it will just seem that way," or, "If it tastes good—you can't eat it."

So the challenge comes (and I'm sure many other dietitians have felt this way)—how can I help all these people?

The motivated people who are ready to change just need guidelines. They grasp the information and make the appropriate changes. Others need to be motivated to see the need for change. Once they understand why it is beneficial to make these changes, they take the information and follow through with the necessary procedures.

Some people are very set in their ways and do not see the importance or need to change their diets. These people are the most challenging and often take longer to convince to change. Some never do. Once people start eating a well-balanced, low-fat diet, they feel better, and this is one of the best motivators to keep on track with their diet.

Sure, we are all human and crave some high-fat or decadent food items, whether they are a hamburger and french fries or that piece of chocolate cheese cake. If consuming these delicacies is kept to a minimum, there is no need to feel guilty. Eat and enjoy. Then get back to following that well-balanced, low-fat diet.

You might ask, "What does a dietitian really tell these people?" After evaluating the nutritional adequacy of their diet, the dietitian gives them recommendations on how to reduce total fat, saturated fats and cholesterol.

Cholesterol is a fatty, wax-like substance found in foods of animal origin, and it is also produced by the body. It is essential for life.

Saturated fats are usually solid at room temperature and can be found in the fat on meats, lard, skin on chicken, butter and other high-fat dairy products (these foods also contain cholesterol). Vegetable oils become saturated by the process of hydrogenation, so watch for these in block margarines, solid shortenings and non-dairy products. Saturated fats also include tropical oils such as coconut oil, palm and palm kernel oil. These saturated fats need to be reduced because they increase blood cholesterol levels.

Polyunsaturated or monounsaturated fats can be used to replace solid fats because they help reduce cholesterol levels when used for this purpose. Polyunsaturated fats are liquid at room temperature and are found in safflower, sunflower, soybean and corn oils. Fish contain a special polyunsaturated fat called Omega-3 fatty acid. Monounsaturated fats are found in canola oil, olives and olive oil, peanuts, avocados and most other nuts. It is important to reduce saturated fats, but it is also necessary to use unsaturated fats sparingly.

TO REDUCE TOTAL FAT, YOU NEED TO FOLLOW A FOLLOW A FEW SIMPLE GUIDELINES:

1. Avoid any fried or deep-fried foods.

2. Add fats sparingly, even when using margarine (soft tub variety), vegetable oils, salad dressings or mayonnaise. Substituting low fat varieties can help reduce fat even further.

3. Watch for hidden fats in baked goods such as cakes, cookies, pies, donuts, croissants, some muffins and crackers. Also avoid high-fat snack foods.

4. Trim the fats from meats, and take the skin off chicken before it is cooked.

5. Use low-fat dairy products.

TO REDUCE SATURATED FATS:

1. Trim fats from the meats, and remove the skin of a chicken.

2. Substitute a butter or lard for a soft tub margarine or a vegetable oil—remember to use these sparingly.

3. Use low-fat dairy products.

THEN TO REDUCE CHOLESTEROL INTAKE:

1. Eat smaller portions of beef, pork, lamb, fish and chicken—all of these contain cholesterol.

2. Limit eggs to two to three per week.

3. Use low-fat dairy products.

Making changes gradually and progressively can help maintain long-term changes. It is important to make these changes a permanent part of a healthier lifestyle, and not to think of them as something you do for only a few months.

Preparing meals at home puts you in control of how much fat, as well as what fat, is used in food preparation. When we are eating in restaurants, it is more difficult to know what to choose. Look for items that are labeled garden fresh, broiled, roasted, poached or steamed in its own juice. If there are any salad dressings, sauces or gravies, always order them on the side, so you can control how much is used. Avoid those items prepared with added fats: anything sauteed, fried, pan-fried or crispy; buttered or in butter sauce; creamed; with gravy or hollandaise; or au gratin, escalloped or marinated in oil. Eating out can be an enjoyable experience, but we can also make it more heart healthy.

I have found that those who adopt the above recommendations, modify other risk factors where possible and get involved in a regular exercise program may lose weight, if needed, and enjoy a healthier lifestyle.

Part of the cardiac rehabilitation program is to bring people back after six months and one year for blood work, a medical examination and a stress test. Those who continue the lifestyle changes show improved cholesterol levels and, in most cases, report a better quality of life and improved exercise levels.

These changes do not come easily, but with the continuation of healthy eating habits, as well as regular exercise, it is my feeling that you are going to enjoy the good life.

Dealing with a Weight Problem

People are considered overweight when they are 10% over their desirable weight, and they are considered obese when they are 20% over. Desirable weights used by the Calgary General Hospital Cardiac Rehabilitation Program are:

Females—100 lbs. (45 kg) for the first 5 feet (152 cm) of height plus five lbs. (2.3 kg) for each inch (2.54 cm) thereafter, plus or minus 10 lbs. (4.5 kg) for frame size.

Males—110 lbs. (45 kg) for the first 5 feet (152 cm) of height plus five lbs. (2.3 kg) for each inch (2.54 cm) thereafter, plus or minus 10 lbs. (4.5 kg) for frame size.

I am six feet tall and weigh about 235 pounds, putting me in the vicinity of 50 lbs. overweight. Just before my surgery, I dropped from 247 to 227 lbs. I gained back approximately 10 lbs. and have levelled off at that point. I joined Lindsay Park in Calgary after I completed my cardiac rehab program, and when I walked three times weekly at a brisk, yet not over-tiring pace, for 45 minutes, I continued to lose approximately one pound a week. Losing weight just from walking has been a subject of controversy, and I have been told that I would also have to change my diet to reach this goal. However, when I was doing this exercise, I don't recall changing eating habits.

Pat Holmes, an exercise specialist at Calgary Cardiac Rehab, recommends that people exercise four to five times a week. The more we exercise, within limits, the quicker we reach our goal. Pat also makes it clear that exercising five times weekly is the maximum; more than this could harm the body.

Some of you may ask, "If you can lose one pound a week by walking on three different occasions for only 45 minutes, why don't you weigh less?" The answer is simple. I, like countless others who are trying to lose weight, do not always follow the routine needed to drop those unwanted pounds. I continually re-evaluate my goal in this regard and strive to establish a pattern that will show permanent results. My goal is to break 200.

For most, eating habits change after heart-related problems. I am one of these, and when I sacrifice all the goodies I enjoy, I put together the following concoction. I eat this at other times also because it is not only weight-reducing, but is delicious and especially enjoyable on cold days. If you try this it, I hope you enjoy it as much as our family does.

CABBAGE SOUP

1 1/4 cups	lean ground beef	570 g
4 cup	beef bouillon	1 L
3 cups	canned tomatoes (diced)	750 mL
2 cups	sliced carrots	500 mL
1 cup	chopped green pepper	250 mL
1 cup	chopped onion	250 mL
1	medium head cabbage, chopped	1
1 tsp.	salt	5 mL
1 tsp.	pepper	5 mL
2 1/2 cups	tomato juice	625 mL
2 cups	celery, chopped	500 mL
1 cup	mushrooms (stems and pieces)	250 mL

Brown the meat in a large soup pot, sprayed with a non-stick spray. Pour off and discard the fat. Add all the other ingredients and cook for at least two hours, making a very concentrated soup. Stir every 20 to 30 minutes. The soup may be served at this point, or it may be frozen in plastic containers; to reheat, add 1/3 cup (75 mL) water or bouillon for each serving.

MICROWAVE INSTRUCTIONS: Brown meat in a plastic colander over a bowl on high for three to five minutes. Discard fat. Combine meat with all other ingredients in a large microwave casserole with a lid. Microwave on medium for 45 minutes, or until vegetables are cooked. Stir every 15 minutes. Microwave only if you are in a hurry as the flavor is enhanced by the long cooking time.

YIELD: 16 servings of 1 cup (250 mL) each, concentrated.

ONE SERVING

		Food Groups
Calories	107	
Protein	9 g	1 1/4 Meat
Fat	4 g	1 Fat
Carbohydrate	8 g	1 Vegetable
Cholesterol	25 mg	
Sodium	597 mg	

See pages 151 to 152, "Reading for Healthy Eating," for a list of books containing recipes that are helpful in reducing cholesterol and/or losing those unwanted pounds.

The Ladies Auxiliary

Each time I visit the Holy Cross Hospital, which is often, I must drop into the concession stand and pick up a lotto 6/49 ticket. I do this because I did it once on a Monday in July, 1991, after I had dropped off a friend, Mike Russell, scheduled for an angiogram. On Thursday morning, after I had checked my numbers on the ticket, which was for the previous night's draw, I found I had five of the six numbers, plus the bonus number, making me an instant winner of $80,892.60! This was an especially happy event for us because I was on disability at the time, and it meant no more mortgage payments. In addition, I was able to give Doug and Barb an unexpected present to help them through life. Marion and I had previously decided not to take a vacation to Waskesiu in Northern Saskatchewan, as we felt it would stretch our budget too far. We had been to Vancouver in June and felt this was our holiday for the year. Needless to say, our plans changed, and I got in another fishing trip to a part of the country where I love to holiday.

The lottery was a bonanza that brought a measure of financial security to my family. But when I remember my windfall as I pass the hospital concession, I am also reminded of a benefit that most people are not aware of and probably never think about. The majority of people you see working in these hospital stands are volunteers, and many of them spend not only countless hours, but many days each month contributing their time for the benefit of others.

All profits earned from these operations are turned over to hospitals for various equipment and for furnishing rooms for the comfort of visitors. These volunteers have helped to furnish one room in the Holy Cross Hospital that visitors to palliative (terminally ill) patients use. It provides individuals in the final chapter of their lives a place to visit with their friends and family in privacy and comfort. One volunteer is Coral MacDonald, a registered nurse who has devoted her life to helping others and who has spent over 25 years at the Holy Cross in this capacity. The next time you have occasion to spend money at one of these outlets, remember that it is going to help this hospital and many others. Also give some thought to the people who work there and the time they unselfishly donate to helping your relatives or friends. With the continuing cutbacks of government monies for medical assistance, this service becomes more important each year.

I discussed my book with Mrs. MacDonald, whom I came to know from visits to her shop, and she agreed to write about the services provided by these volunteers:

Hospital auxiliaries have always played a role in the development of hospitals. They may not have been, at times, identified as auxiliaries, but rather as ladies aid or guilds. Regardless of their title, they were formed by groups of women, working together, initiated ways and means to raise money or collect various materials required in the day-to-day operation of a hospital. They did, in earlier days, go door-to-door for monetary contributions or everyday items of use to patients, such as linens, furnishings and dishes.

In pioneer days, without the services provided by these volunteers, many of our hospitals would not have been able to survive. These women not only performed the services mentioned above, but would often do the cleaning, help with meal preparation, and at times, even provide nursing care.

Today, hospital auxiliaries continue to do much the same type of work, but usually in much more modern surroundings. Their role now is to assist where necessary in providing services required to give each patient the best care possible.

As hospital budgets continue to be cut back, auxiliaries are often asked to provide equipment, furnishings and other materials not provided for in the budgets. These include requests, which are varied and many, for heart monitors, fetal monitors, video cameras, surgical instruments, microwave ovens, rocking chairs, furnishings for waiting rooms and even hair curlers.

Donations vary from $300 to $500 up to $500,000 annually to respective hospitals. Nearly all communities have enjoyed the "Strawberry Teas" and "Rummage Sales," many of the women going home with their own rummage—sold and bought once again.

One time I was visiting the Peace River Hospital Auxiliary and was taken to visit an elderly Native who had not seen her family for quite some time. She was certain that I was going to have some moose meat for her. After quite a scramble around Peace River we were able to come up with some—a "patient comfort," in this instance supplied by the Ladies Auxiliary.

Today, our auxiliary has become more sophisticated as we now run gift shops, tuck shops, beauty parlors and coffee shops. In the ever-changing health care field, we found that we must become more business orientated, without losing our goal to provide patients with the extra comforts they need.

We continue to be volunteers, firm in our belief that we fill a much-needed role in the modern health care system.

Straight from the Heart

Here I am, at the end of my story. It's been a fun time and a frustrating time writing this book, and to say that I am finally finished gives me both happy and sad feelings.

It was fun because during the course of writing, I have had the opportunity to talk with new people and to get to know previous acquaintances better. They have certainly enriched my life.

It was frustrating because sometimes, during the course of these writings, I have found it difficult to convey my exact feelings, so that the reader would understand them. I wondered if I could have expressed myself in a different way, yet didn't know quite how, or if I had written something but hadn't managed to send the message I intended.

It was also disheartening at times to receive the necessary critical feedback on this book because it made the task seem even more daunting. However, hundreds of hours of research went into this project to ensure medical accuracy even though I am not part of this profession, and every effort was made to perfect the final volume. This included professional substantive and technical editing by the most suitable people. I hope now that you can read and appreciate this book simply for what it is—a help to those who need it.

Another frustration I experienced was that I lost the complete book off my computer after typing about eight chapters. I was a novice on the computer before starting this book, but it didn't take very long to learn the advantage of saving my work on a floppy diskette. It took many tedious hours to rewrite the manuscript.

In a way, I'm almost sad to be finished because it was such an exuberating experience to do all the things I never imagined doing before tackling such a project. Now that I am finished, I sometimes wonder what I will do to keep myself occupied, but already thoughts are creeping into my mind—maybe another book? It's sure to be a best-seller if I can convince all my immediate family's offspring to buy one copy each.

During the course of these writings, I have, at times, turned my thoughts to God and, as mentioned previously, He has been around and there when I needed Him. With the exception of my early childhood, I have never been much of a church-going person, but hopefully these are not the credentials I need when I meet this Divine Being.

Both Miss Stewart and Dr. Kieser commented on pages 17 to 20 that they enjoyed reading *Straight From The Heart*. They also mentioned that this book offered reassurance to people going through cardiac-related experiences and to their families and friends. In their day-to-day work, both these medical professionals are constantly in contact with such people, and are in a position to recognize the advantages of providing emotional and intellectual support during an extremely trying period. If you are a cardiac patient or know someone who is, I hope that you have benefited by reading *Straight from the Heart,* and that it has, during your periods of anxiety and despair, brought you some of this emotional and intellectual support.

ENJOY A WELL-BALANCED MEAL

Reading for Healthy Eating

The following list of cookbooks is, with the exception of the third, from the *Resource Manual of Nutrition Month, 1990.* This information is being passed on to you in the hope that you will find enjoyable meals that will not only be nourishing, but help you with problems you have with your eating habits. This list was included with literature I received while attending the Cardiac Rehab program at the Calgary General Hospital.

1. *Eat Well, Live Well,* H. Bishop MacDonald and M. Howards, Macmillan of Canada, 1990.

2. *Light-Hearted Cookbook,* A. Lindsay, Key Porter Books, Don Mills, ON, 1987.

3. *Light-Hearted Everyday Cookbook,* A. Lindsay, Macmillan of Canada, Toronto, ON, 1991.

4. *Eating for the Health of It,* H. Bishop MacDonald, Hounslow Press, Willowdale, ON.

5. *Jane Brody's Nutrition Book: A Lifetime Guide to Good Eating for Better Health and Weight Control,* J. Brody, W. W. Norton, New York, NY, 1986.

6. *Nutrition for the Prime of Your Life,* A. Natow and J. A. Heslin, McGraw Hill, Toronto, ON, 1984.

7. *Thirty Days to Better Nutrition.* V. Aronson, Doubleday, New York, NY, 1984.

8. *The Fast Food Guide,* M. Jacobson and S. Fritschner, Workman Publishing, New York, NY, 1986.

9. *Smart Cooking,* A. Lindsay, MacMillan of Canada, Toronto, ON, 1986.

10. *The Enlightened Eater,* M. Kane and R. Schwartz, Methuen Publishing, Toronto, ON, 1987.

11. *Jane Brody's Good Food Book, Living the High Carbohydrate Way,* J. Brody, W. W. Norton, New York, NY, 1985.

12. *Light and Easy Choices,* Kay Spicer, Grosvenor House, Toronto, ON, 1985.

13. *Choice Cooking,* Canadian Diabetes Association, N. C. Press, Toronto, ON, 1982.

14. *Don't Eat Your Heart Out Cookbook,* J. Piscatella, Workman Publishing, New York, NY, 1983.

15. *American Heart Association Cookbook,* Balantine Books, New York, NY, 1986.

16. *The Total Fibre Book,* M. Fraser, H. Bishop MacDonald, Grosvenor House, Toronto, ON, 1987.

17. *The Moosewood Cookbook,* Allergy Information Association, Methuen Publishing, Toronto, ON, 1983.

18. *The New Laurel's Kitchen,* L. Robertson, C. Flinders and B. Godfrey, Ten Speed Press, Berleley. CA, 1986.

Warning Signs

Beating the odds against these two killers means being able to recognize the early warning signs. Be on the lookout for:

HEART ATTACK

1. Heavy pressure, discomfort, burning or a squeezing sensation in the center of the chest.

2. Pain may spread to arms or neck and may come and go.

3. Shortness of breath.

4. Nausea, vomiting or indigestion.

Weakness, fatigue, greyish skin color.

STROKE

1. Sudden weakness or numbness of the face, arm or leg on one side of the body.

2. Loss of speech, or trouble in speaking or in understanding speech.

3. Unexplained dizziness, unsteadiness or sudden falls.

4. Dimness, loss of vision or double vision in one eye.

IF YOU EXPERIENCE THESE SYMPTOMS, TELL SOMEONE ELSE IMMEDIATELY.

IF YOU NOTE THESE SYMPTOMS IN SOMEONE ELSE:

1. Take charge. The victim will likely deny what is happening.

2. Insist that the victim stop all activity and sit or lie down.

3. Ask if the victim is being treated for heart attack or stroke. If so, help with medication.

4. Call your local emergency number.

5. Get the victim to the nearest hospital.

YOU MUST ACT IMMEDIATELY! HALF OF ALL HEART ATTACK DEATHS OCCUR BEFORE THE VICTIM GETS TO HOSPITAL.

SOURCE: The Heart and Stroke Foundation of Canada

Cardiac Commentary

ACUTE—an illness that has a severe but relatively short course.

ANEURYSM—a permanent swelling of an artery due to weakness in its wall by disease, an abnormality present at birth or traumatic injury.

ANGINA (angina pectoris)—medical term for a pain, usually in the chest, but can occur in the jaw, gums or throat. At times there may be just an aching or numbness in the wrist or arm. Caused by a temporary difference between the supply and demand of oxygen to the heart.

ANGIOGRAM—described on pages 52 to 54.

ANGIOPLASTY—described on pages 60 to 63.

ANOXIA—a total lack of oxygen.

ANTICOAGULANT—any substance that prevents blood clotting. Some drugs that perform this function are heparin, coumadin and warfarin.

ARRYTHMIA (or DYSRHYTHMIA)—an abnormal rhythm of the heart.

ARTERIOSCLEROSIS—commonly called hardening of the arteries, includes a variety of conditions that cause artery walls to thicken and lose elasticity.

ARTERY—any one of a series of blood vessels that carry

blood from the heart to the various parts of the body. Arteries have thick, elastic walls that can expand as blood flows through them.

ATHEROSCLEROSIS—a form of arteriosclerosis in which the inner layers of artery walls are made thick and irregular by deposits of a fatty substance. These deposits (called atheromata or plaques) project above the surface of the inner layer of the artery, and thus decrease the diameter of the internal channel of the vessel.

BLOOD PRESSURE—the pressure exerted by the flow of blood through the main arteries. Blood pressure rises and falls as the heart responds to the varying demands made by the body during different activities, such as exercise, stress and sleep. This pressure is strongest when the heart contracts to squeeze blood out into the arteries (systolic reading). Pressure is lowest between heart beats, when the heart rests and refills with blood before contracting again (diastolic reading). Blood pressure is generally expressed by two numbers (e.g. 120/80—the first representing the systolic pressure and the second the diastolic pressure).

BRADYCARDIA—an abnormally slow heartbeat.

CARDIAC—pertaining to the heart.

CARDIAC ARREST—when the heart stops beating.

CARDIOPULMONARY RESUSCITATION (CPR)—an emergency measure used to artificially maintain a person's breathing and heartbeat in the event these functions suddenly stop. CPR consists of keeping the airway open and performing mouth to mouth breathing and external heart massage to keep oxygenated blood circulating through the body.

CARDIOVASCULAR—pertaining to the heart and blood vessels.

CATHETERIZATION—the process of examining the heart by introducing a thin tube (catheter) into a vein or artery and passing it into the heart.

CEREBRAL HEMORRHAGE—bleeding within the brain caused by rupture of a blood vessel.

CEREBRAL THROMBOSIS—formation of a blood clot in an artery in the brain. The clot may completely block the artery, cutting off the supply of blood, nutrients and oxygen to a region of the brain, causing a stroke.

CHOLESTEROL—a steroid-like chemical present in some foods, notably animal fats, eggs and dairy products. An over-high level of cholesterol in the blood is associated with atherosclerosis. Some amount of cholesterol in the body is necessary for healthy functioning.

CONGENITAL—a disease or condition that is present at birth.

CONGESTIVE—a term applied to heart failure when both left and right sides of the heart are affected.

CORONARY ARTERY DISEASE—conditions that cause narrowing of the coronary arteries so blood flow to the heart muscle is reduced.

CORONARY HEART DISEASE—damage to the heart muscle due to insufficient flow of blood through the coronary arteries.

CORONARY OCCLUSION—complete obstruction of one of the coronary arteries that hinders blood flow to some part of the heart muscle, usually from progressive atherosclerosis.

CORONARY THROMBOSIS—development of a clot in a coronary artery.

CYANOSIS—blueness of skin caused by insufficient oxygen in the blood. The condition can be caused by respiratory or heart problems, and is often a sign of serious illness.

DIABETES—a disease in which the body is unable to use sugar, normally owing to insufficient amounts of insulin, normally produced by the pancreas. Diabetes may lead to coronary artery disease and heart attack, because the extra sugar has a tendency to deposit itself on the interior wall of the arteries.

DIASTOLIC BLOOD PRESSURE—the lowest blood pressure measured in the arteries, it occurs when the heart muscle is relaxed between beats.

EMBOLUS—a clot or other plug brought by the blood from another vessel and forced into a smaller one, thus obstructing the circulation.

HEART ATTACK—occurs when an obstruction in one of the coronary arteries prevents an adequate supply of oxygen to the heart, which results in death of a portion of the heart muscle.

ISCHEMIA—decreased blood flow to an organ, usually due to constriction or obstruction of an artery.

LIPID—a fatty substance insoluble in blood.

NITROGLYCERIN—a drug that causes blood vessels to expand. Used in treating angina pectoris.

OBESITY—see page 142.

PALPITATION—a situation that occurs when the heart is beating irregularly, more strongly, or more rapidly than usual.

PHLEBITIS—inflammation of a vein, often accompanied by clot formation. The preferred medical name for this condition is thrombophlebitis.

PERICARDIUM—the outer "sac" that surrounds the heart.

PERICARDITIS—inflammation of the outer membrane surrounding the heart.

RHEUMATIC FEVER—a disease, usually occurring in childhood, that may follow a few weeks after a streptococcal infection. In some cases the infection affects the heart and results in scarring of the valves, weakening the heart muscle, or damaging the sac enclosing the heart.

STROKE—see cerebral thrombosis.

SYSTOLIC BLOOD PRESSURE—the highest blood pressure measured in the arteries. It occurs when the heart contracts with each heartbeat.

TRIGLYCERIDE—one type of fat or lipid present in the blood and body tissues.

Straight from the Heart

To write this story
Straight from the heart
Was a challenge to finish
Yet harder to start

But once I began
And with the support
Of people who cared
I formed this report

As I got more help
From those in the know
I was determined to finish
From a start that was slow

The time and effort
Given freely by those
Made it more pleasant
With these people I chose

Three doctors assisted
Took time from their day
To add expertise
In a medical way

There also was help
From nurses who shared
Their cardiac knowledge
With those who cared

I also discovered
As I wrote this report
That my family was there
With love and support

There are others who gave
The help I did need
I want to thank all
For this generous deed

After getting their comments
I developed a feeling
That this was a book
You would find appealing

It was meant to portray
For the heart how to care
I'm sure you will find
That this message is there

After reading the story
You will no doubt see
The efforts contributed
By others than me

When then you think
Of various people in life
There are so many out there
To help you with strife

I want you to know
That there are those who care
And also from above
There's help with a prayer